THE PRESIDENT
AND THE PRESIDENCY

THE PRESIDENT
AND THE PRESIDENCY

BY LOUIS BROWNLOW

55714

PUBLIC ADMINISTRATION SERVICE

Chicago : 1949

PRINTED IN THE UNITED STATES OF AMERICA
THE LAKESIDE PRESS, R. R. DONNELLEY & SONS COMPANY
CHICAGO, ILLINOIS, AND CRAWFORDSVILLE, INDIANA

Foreword

THE WALGREEN FOUNDATION for the study of American Institutions was established at the University of Chicago through the generosity of the late Charles R. Walgreen. The present work constitutes one of a series of volumes based upon lectures presented before the student body of the University of Chicago. Given by leading scholars and men in public life, each series deals either practically or theoretically with some aspect of American institutions.

Mr. Louis Brownlow, the author of this series, has had a distinguished career in American public affairs. As journalist, as Commissioner of the District of Columbia, as city manager, as Director of the Public Administration Clearing House, as keen and penetrating student of politics and administration, as friend and adviser to Presidents, he has had a rich experience in the life of the nation. From that experience he has drawn the material for this volume.

JEROME G. KERWIN
Chairman, Walgreen Foundation

Preface

In April, 1947, I gave a series of six lectures under the sponsorship of the Charles R. Walgreen Foundation at the University of Chicago on the subject, "The President and the Presidency." Now that more than two years have elapsed since these lectures were spoken, it has been decided to publish them. During the time intervening between the spoken word and the preparation for printing, many things happened that now are clear to my hindsight, but which were veiled to my foresight.

A tremendous number of things would affect in greater or less degree what I might say on the subject of the President and the Presidency if I were talking in the summer of 1949 instead of the spring of 1947. First and foremost among these things that happened was, of course, the Presidential election of 1948. That event in itself carried in its train many happenings of related import.

Faced with the problem, after this lapse of time, of preparing the spoken lectures for publication, it seemed to me that I had three choices.

One was to do the speeches over again in the light of my present knowledge. To have done that would have been to change from the spoken to the written word. This would have compelled me to turn from consultation of my memory, reinforced by slight reading, to a task in historical research for which I have no taste. It would, in any case, have obliged me to depart from my original purpose of talking about the President and the Presidency, and to go into a subject I wished to avoid—the conflicts and frictions among the three great branches of the American government.

Another course which I considered was the writing of a postscript in which I would attempt to set down what I might think to be some of the more significant happenings of the biennium that has elapsed since I gave voice to the more or less random thoughts recorded in these six lectures. That would have required, however, a survey, necessarily myopic, which could have been put down only in the form of a journalistic review of the last two years of American high politics. As contrasted with the 158 years of the Presidency encompassed in the spoken lectures, such a review necessarily would have been out of scale in length and out of proportion in emphasis, and could have resulted in nothing but distortion.

A third choice was to print the lectures as they were spoken, with only such changes as editors require to bolster their prejudice in favor of what they consider the king's English and with an occasional gesture of deference to authority in the form of a footnote. This scheme would leave the reader, if such there should be, free to fill in his own notions of what happened between the spring of '47 and the summer of '49. He will discover that I was then uncertain whether any Republican nominee for the Presidency ever could be renominated after a defeat. None ever had been before. But Mr. Dewey was in '48. He will discover that I did not know whether or not a Vice President succeeding to the Presidency could gain party support for reelection. John Tyler, Millard Fillmore, Andrew Johnson, and Chester A. Arthur had not been able to do so. Theodore Roosevelt and Calvin Coolidge had. I asked the question whether Harry Truman could or could not gain such support. He did. When, as I spoke these words, I made low bows in the direction of the pollsters as rivals of the ballot boxes, none of my auditors seemed to disagree with me. I was as wrong as were, apparently, my hearers. And I talked too confidently about a two-party system when a four-party election was just over the hill.

But I have resisted the temptation to change the text.

The outstanding event of the time was a political triumph for the incumbent President; a triumph that lost no glory because it was wholly unexpected by the great majority of political observers; a triumph that added luster to the institution of the Presidency because it was so peculiarly and personally a triumph of the President himself.

During these same two years a series of developing problems of constantly increasing importance in international affairs has tended to strengthen the Presidency as an institution for the simple reason that from day to day the concern of the American people in foreign affairs has become relatively greater than in domestic affairs. That the President is charged with the initiative in international business no one questions. Wide and deep as may be the differences in domestic affairs, as expressed in party politics, economic and social programs, and varying philosophies of the people of the country and their representatives in the Congress, there is a tendency to compose these differences and unite behind the President in international affairs. More and more, so indicates the trend, politics stops at the water's edge.

At the same time, nothing has become more evident in these two years than the simple fact that the President is a democratic leader, not an absolute dictator; he does not have things his own way.

The years from 1947 to 1949 were marked not only by President Truman's personal victory in the election of 1948, not only by the increasing solidarity of public support for his foreign policy, but also by increasing difficulties with the Congress; by a double revolt in the Democratic Party, of which he was assumed to be the leader, which introduced two new parties into the campaign fray; and by the emergence of new conflicts with respect to what should be the program of the nation.

And yet it is clear that public opinion continues to hold the President responsible for the general guidance of the nation's affairs, its political management, its economic health, and its security from enemies both foreign and domestic. It is clear, too, that it is difficult for him to measure up to these responsibilities unless he has the support of a majority in both Houses of the Congress, reinforced by party discipline. It is also evident that the President needs help if he is to live up to what the people expect of him.

To the current discussions of our difficult problems that center on the man in the White House, I hope that these antiquarian observations may be of some little interest.

I should like to acknowledge with gratitude the help that I had from Miss Louise Eaton in transposing the notes of the spoken word into written form, and the editorial assistance given to me by Mr. Sidney Hyman and Mr. Farrell Symons.

Louis Brownlow

Contents

THE PRESIDENT
AND THE PRESIDENCY

The Presidency: An American Institution

AT THE VERY BEGINNING, may I say that the title of this series of lectures, "The President and the Presidency," gives rise to some apprehension on my part lest it be supposed that I plan to cover the subject in any thorough or systematic way. To do this would involve not only the recital but the critical analysis of most of the history of the United States, and not only its political and military history, but its economic, social, and cultural history as well. Obviously this is a task too vast for a series of six spoken lectures—even if it were not, as it is, far beyond my powers.

I intend in these lectures to look at the Presidency as a unique and peculiarly American institution devised by both law and custom; to examine the attributes of the office, how the men who fill it are chosen, what is expected of them, how they are controlled, and how they are equipped for the task; and to try to determine what help the President requires if he is to meet what is expected of him.

Two recurrent points of emphasis will appear in all this. First, I mean to consider the institutional aspects of the Presidency as they have appeared, for the most part, after 1900. And I choose that date not at random, but because the Presidency as an *institution* emerged in its modern phase with the succession of Theodore Roosevelt to office following McKinley's assassination. The Presidency was certainly of supreme importance in the foundation of the government under the Constitution, in the expansion of our national domain, and in the preservation of the

Union. Yet I hold that for all these tremendous activities in earlier times, the Presidency as an *institution* did not equal what it has become since 1900 in the scope of its activities, the breadth of its influence, or the complexity of the problems with which it deals.

The second point of emphasis will be this: I shall consider how the Presidents have affected the Presidency, changing it from time to time in the light of their own personalities; and how the Presidency seems to have affected the Presidents, molding and sometimes reshaping them into entirely different persons from what they seemed to be when they first undertook their duties. If I take the two phases, the President and the Presidency, the Man and the Institution, together, it is because, as I see it, while they are distinguishable at certain times and in the light of certain events, they are nevertheless inseparable. The man in the White House cannot be looked at except in the framework of his office, and the exalted position he occupies cannot be appraised except in terms of the men who have held it.

These lectures are based not on profound or extensive research, but rather on my own observations and reflections, refreshed by some selective reading. In their preparation I have relied largely on my memory—which, of course, is frequently imperfect—of what I have seen, and on what has been left in my mind from scores of conversations and some hundreds of political discussions and arguments stretching over many years. I own to an intense interest in politics, an interest which carries me back to the Presidential campaign of 1884, when I was but five years old: I was a member of a county political party committee when I was twelve; I held what was then regarded as a political public office when I was fourteen; I was an editor of a partisan political country paper when I was fifteen; I became a political reporter on a daily newspaper at twenty-one; and at twenty-five I went to Washington as a newspaper correspondent.

These youthful adventures in politics have no place here and I mention them in passing only to indicate how long I have had a reason for considering my subject, which is the very apex of American politics.

From that day, April 30, in 1789, in New York, after the first Congress elected under the Constitution had spent about two months trying to get a quorum together in order to count the votes to determine who should be the first President of the United States, to the day in January, 1949, when President Truman's term expires, there will have elapsed a period of one hundred and sixty years. During that time there have been thirty-two Presidents. All but the first have lived in Washington in that first of buildings to be erected in the new National Capital—the Presidential Palace, it was called then: later it became the Executive Mansion, and in my day in Washington, by fiat of Theodore Roosevelt, it became the White House. Late in February, 1904, I, a newly arrived correspondent of two southern newspapers, the *Nashville Banner* and the *Louisville Evening Post,* sat down in the Cabinet Room in the White House for my first talk with a President of the United States. He was the first of eight Presidents I have known—most of them very slightly indeed; a few of them quite well.

Thus, during a quarter of the time of the existence of the Presidency, I have known or at least I have met one-fourth of all the Presidents, and have had this personal contact to sustain my early interest—an interest that was in no wise diminished by my work as a journalist or, later, as a public administrator. I must admit that I was somewhat startled when I first realized, as I did but a few weeks ago, that when I had my first interview with President Theodore Roosevelt in the White House we were then nearer in point of time to Abraham Lincoln than we were to Harry Truman.

Mr. Lincoln, who from our own date in history stood at a

mid-point in the Presidency, paid tribute to the country's fifteen previous Presidents by saying of them in his first inaugural address: "They have conducted it through many perils, and generally with great success." The word "generally," it has recently been pointed out, originally read "on the whole," and was changed by Lincoln at Seward's suggestion.[1] The shading between these words may seem of no great importance to us now, but Lincoln must have packed the sentence with meaning in the way of qualification, for he undoubtedly classified some of his predecessors as strong, some as weak, and he probably classified some of them as right and some as wrong.

Though history is silent on the point, it seems reasonable to conclude that Lincoln changed his mind about some of his predecessors once he began his own duties as President. It is most probable, for instance, that he revised his estimate of President James K. Polk. Fourteen years earlier, as a Congressman from Illinois, Lincoln had been sharply critical of Polk, not only in his capacity as head of the administration, but also in his role as Commander-in-Chief of the Armed Forces during the Mexican War. Being exposed in his own day to the kind of criticism he had leveled at Polk, Lincoln, as a wartime President, may well have taken a more sympathetic view of the problems Polk faced and the manner in which he handled them. All this, of course, is conjecture, for there is no direct statement by Lincoln to support such a belief.

Appraisals of this sort have sometimes been made by one President of his several predecessors, and they reveal as much about the judge as the men he judged. It would be still more interesting if we could have one appraisal written by a President when he was merely a candidate for the office or at the beginning of his term, and then a second appraisal by him of his

---

[1] *Lincoln's War Cabinet,* by Burton J. Hendrick. Boston: Little, Brown & Co., 1946, p. 150.

predecessors at the end of his own term. I am certain that the contrast between the two estimates would provide rich material on the sobering effects of responsibility.

In the modern phase of the Presidency, history is more rewarding in the record it offers of how another President, Theodore Roosevelt, came to change his mind about some of his predecessors. In his youth Theodore Roosevelt had denounced Andrew Jackson as a demagogue, if not a "dangerous" one. But then came Roosevelt's own rise to power and its companion responsibilities. Once in the White House, he took a second look at Jackson, and as a result elevated him to a place beside Lincoln and but a shade below the great Washington. Though I shall refer in a moment to the broad categories into which Theodore Roosevelt grouped his predecessors, the measuring stick he applied to the Presidents comes out by inference from a self-appraisal. In his *Autobiography*,[2] Roosevelt wrote:

The most important factor in getting the right spirit in my Administration, next to the insistence upon courage, honesty, and a genuine democracy of desire to serve the plain people, was my insistence upon the theory that the executive power was limited only by specific restrictions and prohibitions appearing in the Constitution or imposed by the Congress under its Constitutional powers. My view was that every executive officer, and above all every executive officer in high position, was a steward of the people bound actively and affirmatively to do all he could for the people, and not to content himself with the negative merit of keeping his talents undamaged in a napkin. I declined to adopt the view that what was imperatively necessary for the Nation could not be done by the President unless he could find some specific authorization to do it. My belief was that it was not only his right but his duty to do anything that the needs of the Nation demanded unless such action was forbidden by the Constitution or by the laws. Under this interpretation of executive power I did and caused to be done many things not previously

---

[2] *Theodore Roosevelt: An Autobiography.* New York: Charles Scribner's Sons, 1913, p. 357.

done by the President and the heads of the departments. I did not usurp power, but I did greatly broaden the use of executive power. In other words, I acted for the public welfare, I acted for the common well-being of all our people, whenever and in whatever manner was necessary, unless prevented by direct constitutional or legislative prohibition. I did not care a rap for the mere form and show of power; I cared immensely for the use that could be made of the substance.

Both Theodore Roosevelt personally, and his concept of the Presidency stated in the passage just quoted, were challenged by William Howard Taft in the course of a series of lectures on "Our Chief Magistrate and His Powers," delivered at Columbia University in 1916. It must be remembered that Taft's challenge may have been tinged by a sense of personal frustration. In 1916, he could look back on almost four years of administration by Woodrow Wilson—four years which he probably believed would have been the second Taft Administration had not Theodore Roosevelt bolted the regular Republican organization. The judicially-minded Taft bore this in mind, for at the beginning of his Columbia lectures he observed:[3] ". . . retirement from office to a place of study and contemplation, rather than of action, modifies somewhat the views formed, *dum fervet opus.*"

He thereupon quoted what Theodore Roosevelt had written about both the nature of the Presidency and his administration of it, and attacked that position in these terms.[4]

My judgment is that the view of . . . Mr. Roosevelt, ascribing an undefined residuum of power to the President is an unsafe doctrine and that it might lead under emergencies to results of an arbitrary character, doing irremediable injustice to private right.

And he said further:[5]

[3] *Our Chief Magistrate and His Powers,* by William Howard Taft. New York: Columbia University Press, 1925 ed., p. 3.
[4] *Ibid.,* p. 144.
[5] *Ibid.,* p. 143 f.

I may add that Mr. Roosevelt, by way of illustrating his meaning as to the differing usefulness of Presidents, divides the Presidents into two classes, and designates them as "Lincoln Presidents" and "Buchanan Presidents." In order more fully to illustrate his division of Presidents on their merits, he places himself in the Lincoln class of Presidents, and me in the Buchanan class. The identification of Mr. Roosevelt with Mr. Lincoln might otherwise have escaped notice, because there are many differences between the two, presumably superficial, which would give the impartial student of history a different impression. It suggests a story which a friend of mine told of his little daughter Mary. As he came walking home after a business day, she ran out from the house to greet him, all aglow with the importance of what she wished to tell him. She said, "Papa, I am the best scholar in the class." The father's heart throbbed with pleasure as he inquired, "Why, Mary, you surprise me. When did the teacher tell you? This afternoon?" "Oh, no," Mary's reply was, "the teacher didn't tell me—I just noticed it myself."

Unfortunately we have, of course, no such appraisals by all Presidents of all their predecessors. That many estimates of this kind were made we cannot doubt, but they must have been revealed, if revealed at all, in casual conversations and for the most part have been lost. All the Presidents with whom I had the pleasure of talking showed an intense interest in their predecessors. Theodore Roosevelt was especially interested in the acts and characters of his Presidential forerunners, and of Lincoln most particularly. And at this point perhaps I may be permitted to introduce a personal recollection that illustrates this point.

When I was the state political correspondent of the *Nashville Banner* around the turn of the century I came to know and admire a charming gentleman, a raconteur of parts, General John T. Wilder, late of the Union Army, then a pioneer ironmaster of Johnson City, Tennessee. Sometime after I arrived in Washington as a correspondent in 1904, and after I had come to know President Roosevelt, General Wilder came to Washington. I knew his Lincoln stories, or some of them, and believed the President would like to hear them. So I made an engagement, which was easy in those days, and took General Wilder to the White House. T. R. had given us an hour. We took two.

General Wilder as a young man in Illinois in 1858 was a very ardent and violent Douglas Democrat. He was tall, full six and six, lean, wiry, alert. One day in 1858 he set out to go to one of the famous debates between Lincoln and Douglas. He told President Roosevelt and me how he got off the "cars" at a railroad crossing—there was no station, no "depot," there, just a crossing—to wait for the train bound for Galesburg, and there he found a man much like himself—very tall, very thin, but older. The older man asked him where he was going. Wilder said he was going to Galesburg to hear the debate.

"Who are you with?"

"I am for Douglas."

"Why?" inquired the stranger.

Wilder told him why he was for Douglas ("freely and at length," said Wilder to us); and then with becoming respect for age asked in turn: "Who are you with?"

To which the other man replied, "I'm for Lincoln," and told him why. When the train came along, young Wilder got on and found in suffusion of embarrassment that he had been debating with Mr. Lincoln himself.

When Lincoln got to the White House, as General Wilder told us the story in the Cabinet Room in the White House some forty-odd years later, he sent for Wilder, who, although an ardent Democrat, was also an equally ardent Union man; and for most of the four years of the war Wilder was an unofficial, unavowed, and always an expendable and disavowable scout from the White House who went about to various army headquarters, various troubled political areas, into all parts of the country and sometimes abroad, to come back from time to time to tell Mr. Lincoln what he had seen and heard. It seems that even at that time there were not only forerunners of the Colonel Houses and the Harry Hopkinses, but also of administrative assistants with a passion for anonymity.

Wilder told President Theodore Roosevelt many stories on that occasion, but the one that the President got the most out of (and when he enjoyed a story the evidence of his enjoyment could be heard for miles around) was this one: Wilder had come in one day from somewhere in the field and was sitting with President Lincoln in an upper room in the White House making his oral report.

Suddenly came the famous phrase "I am reminded," and Mr. Lincoln said: "You may not know it, but I taught school, for a little while, in a log cabin school house with split logs for seats. I couldn't teach much. The 'scholars,' about a dozen, ranged in age from six to sixteen. For reading the only book we had was the Bible. The whole school was one class in reading, and they'd come up to me and read, verse and verse about, in rotation. The little boys and girls were nearly all about seven, eight, or nine years old. But there were older ones too, and one of them was a dull-witted sixteen-year-old named Willy, who was as tall as I was—a great, stumbling, awkward fellow.

"As we were reading along, the little boys and girls picked up every verse, rattling off with easy precision the memorized, oft repeated text. But Willy found it very difficult to read. I had almost physically to lift him over it, not only word by word but syllable by syllable. At last we got to the story of the fiery furnace and the particular verse about Shadrach, Meshach, and Abednego. Slowly and painfully we got over it. Then the little girl next in order picked up the following verse and rattled it off. Willy began to bawl. 'Willy,' I said, 'what's the matter?' 'Teacher,' he says, 'I counted down the verses here, and here come them three damn fellers again.'"

At that—so General Wilder told Theodore Roosevelt—Mr. Lincoln looked out the window and pointed to three men coming up the walk, Charles Sumner, Ben Wade, and Thad Stevens—three men who as leaders of an antiadministration clique in the Congress were making his life miserable. T. R. did not miss the point.

Woodrow Wilson, the student, the teacher, and the writer who succeeded Taft, left in print an appraisal of sorts of most of those who had preceded him. To Washington and Lincoln he gave the highest meed of praise. Yet even Wilson's views of his predecessors underwent a change once he himself occupied the White House. In 1910, two years before his election, he told me that his most considered judgments and deepest convictions were to be found in his volume of essays, entitled, *Mere Literature*.[6] Reading there, you find that Wilson viewed Washington as one of a group of great rebel Englishmen (as he undoubtedly was); Jefferson was too much under the spell of France and the French Deists for a Presbyterian parson's son; Jackson is set down as a great westerner; and Lincoln was emerging in Wilson's thought as the first great American. But once in the White House, Woodrow Wilson turned more and more to Jefferson and to Jackson for his doctrine, discovering even a relationship between his favorite mentor, Jeremy Bentham, and Old Hickory that went deeper than their somewhat casual exchange of letters.[7] But Lincoln continued to be Wilson's hero—perhaps because Lincoln found in the Constitution what a President should be able to find in it: the means to save a nation.

Franklin D. Roosevelt did not live to write what he thought or to record what undoubtedly were his changing and shifting estimates of his forerunners. But, when the Cabinet Room was remodeled and redecorated in his time, the visitor might have

[6] *Mere Literature and Other Essays,* by Woodrow Wilson. Boston: Houghton Mifflin Co., 1896.
[7] *The Works of Jeremy Bentham.* Edinburgh: W. Tait, 1843, Vol. XI, pp. 39–42.

been justified in deducing a certain emphasis given to the Presidency as a political force in a democracy operating through political parties. In the new Cabinet Room hung but three portraits—all of them of Democratic Presidents: Thomas Jefferson, Andrew Jackson, and Woodrow Wilson. At the same time, it should be said that the names of others—Lincoln and "Uncle Ted" and "Old Grover"—were ever on his tongue and their examples always in his mind, as members of his Cabinet and others with whom he discussed his problems can testify.

Of course, his predecessors whom he had known best were Theodore Roosevelt, his fifth cousin and the uncle of his wife, a kinsman who engaged his admiration and unquestionably had a large share in kindling his own political ambition; and Woodrow Wilson, under whose Presidency he had served as Assistant Secretary of the Navy and with whom he had frequent personal contacts. Franklin Roosevelt spoke often of "Uncle Ted" or "T. R." He spoke often, too, of "President Wilson," sometimes of "Mr. Wilson," sometimes of merely "Wilson," but usually of "President Wilson." To no other of his forerunners did he, in my hearing, accord the high title, "President." Some of the friends of Franklin Roosevelt have said that Wilson was his principal hero. Two or three persons who were very close to him in the White House have given an odd and indirect confirmation to this by telling me that F.D.R. never made the same mistakes as Woodrow Wilson—he had studied him too closely.

Of all the Presidents from 1900 on, I am certain that Theodore Roosevelt, Woodrow Wilson, and Franklin D. Roosevelt always kept in mind what their forerunners had said and done. All three of these men had a quick sensitivity for history. The first two wrote it, all three consciously lived it while it was unfolding, and the third one was cut off before his plans, made on a vast scale, for collecting the history of his time could be real-

ized. Each of these three men was in some degree affected by the
men who held the office before him; each of the three was in
some degree changed by the office—which may be equally true
in varying degrees of all thirty-two Presidents in our history.
Out of the historical sense of these three men, joined and heightened as they were by the tremendous changes that occurred in
their external environment, there has come into being a deepen-
ing tradition of the institution of the Presidency which affects,
sometimes positively, and no doubt negatively, the thinking of
any man who is the President for the time being.

The views held by the rest of us on Presidents and the Presidency are, of course, available in bulk. And they form a very
complex and often confusing portrait—which, again, is by no
means static, but is in a constant state of flux. In 1937 the President's Committee on Administrative Management, the members
of which were Charles E. Merriam, Luther Gulick, and myself,
set down its views on the attributes of the Presidency and the
obligations of the man who fills that office. We wrote:[8]

> Our Presidency unites at least three important functions. From one
> point of view the President is a political leader—leader of a party,
> leader of the Congress, leader of a people. From another point of
> view he is head of the Nation in the ceremonial sense of the term, the
> symbol of our American national solidarity. From still another point
> of view the President is the Chief Executive and administrator within
> the Federal system and service. In many types of government these
> duties are divided or only in part combined, but in the United States
> they have always been united in one and the same person whose
> duty it is to perform all of these tasks.

This was written in December, 1936. In reading these words
now, I think it a little odd that we should have omitted from that
paragraph any reference to the President as the Commander-in-

---

[8] *Administrative Management in the Government of the United States:* Report of
the President's Committee on Administrative Management. Washington: Government
Printing Office, 1937.

Chief of the Armed Forces of the Nation. We certainly were not
insensitive to the voices that were stridently declaring that
democracy was done. Nor were we unaware of the struggle that
was at that moment taking place in Spain. The omission of any
mention of the President as Commander-in-Chief was due, I
think, simply to the fact that we were concerned in our report
with an attempt to improve the machinery available to the
President as an *administrator*. As a matter of fact, the sentence
immediately preceding that paragraph is an index not only to
American thought and practice as it had developed up until
1935, but a very prophecy of how the peculiarly and uniquely
American institution of the Presidency was destined to still those
same strident scoffers. It reads:[9] "The American Executive as
an institution stands across the path of those who mistakenly
assert that democracy must fail because it can neither decide
promptly nor act vigorously." Another democracy also stood
across that path because it could decide promptly and act vigorously—the British nation, with its flexible constitution which
enables it to mass and consolidate the executive power to meet
the challenge of a crisis.

Our fuller catalog of the attributes of the Presidency was contained in the following paragraphs from that same report of the
President's Committee,[9] from which I quote again, but this time
with due acknowledgment to Dr. Charles E. Merriam who
wrote the paragraphs:

The need for action in realizing democracy was as great in 1789
as it is today. It was thus not by accident but by deliberate design
that the founding fathers set the American Executive in the Constitution on a solid foundation. Sad experience under the Articles of
Confederation, with an almost headless Government and committee
management, had brought the American Republic to the edge of
ruin. Our forefathers had broken away from hereditary government

[9] *Ibid.*

and pinned their faith on democratic rule, but they had not found a way to equip the new democracy for action. Consequently, there was grim purpose in resolutely providing for a Presidency which was to be a national office. The President is indeed the one and only national officer representative of the entire Nation. There was hesitation on the part of some timid souls in providing the President with an election independent of the Congress; with a longer term than most governors of that day; with the duty of informing the Congress as to the state of the Union and of recommending to its consideration "such Measures as he shall judge necessary and expedient"; with a two-thirds veto; with a wide power of appointment; and with military and diplomatic authority. But this reluctance was overcome in the face of need and a democratic executive established.

Equipped with these broad constitutional powers, reenforced by statute, by custom, by general consent, the American Executive must be regarded as one of the very greatest contributions made by our Nation to the development of modern democracy—a unique institution the value of which is as evident in times of stress and strain as in periods of quiet.

One cannot find, however, in this or in any other place that I know, a listing of the attributes of the Presidency upon which all students and observers are agreed. Some will stress one phase of Presidential powers; others will emphasize an aspect of its obligations. In 1944, for example, Mr. George Fort Milton wrote: "In the one hundred and fifty-five years since George Washington took the oath . . . the President of the United States of America has become the principal representative of the will of the people of the most powerful democracy in the world." [10] This has been done, Mr. Milton says, by "Constitution, crisis and custom, the great architects of our political institutions," imposing on the President six types of public service. The President, he says, is Chief of State, Chief of Foreign Relations, Commander-in-Chief of the Armed Forces,

---

[10] *The Use of Presidential Power: 1789–1943,* by George Fort Milton. Boston: Little, Brown & Co., 1944, p. 3.

Chief of Government, Chief of Party, and spokesman of public opinion.[11]

This difference in stress and emphasis can be heard among people everywhere, and the same persons do not stress the same things at all times. Thus, during the late war, almost everybody heard someone praise President Roosevelt as a war leader and at the same time condemn him for a domestic demagogue; or another who praised both his military and domestic policies but deplored his party affiliation; or still another who approved his conduct of foreign relations but doubted the wisdom of his direct control of military strategy; and so on.

Oddly enough, all of this seeming double-talk has a kind of Constitutional basis. The Constitution assigns so many roles to the President that it is difficult to arrive at a single, simple, all-inclusive definition of his powers, duties, and obligations. Yet for all the difficulty which besets any effort to define the nature of the Presidency or a President as a political entity in itself, the undertaking becomes incredibly complicated when the definition is attempted in terms of the separation of powers between the Executive, Legislative, and Judicial Branches of Government set up by the Constitution.

The theory of separation of powers on which the Constitution is based, the principle of checks and balances enshrined in it, made it inevitable that when differences of opinion developed among the three branches, each would appeal to the Constitution as justification for its action in the instant case. Each would appeal to the Constitution to prove that the other party to the conflict was attempting to subvert the essential principles of the government. Thus, when in a particular time and on a particular issue persons disagree with the President, they are apt to say that he is usurping the power of the Congress; or when they disapprove of legislation enacted by the Congress, turn to the

[11] *Ibid.*, p. 3 f.

Supreme Court to invalidate it; or when the Congress and the Courts seem too slow in solving an urgent problem, turn to the President and demand that he give them what they want forthwith.

The catalog of factors that make for complexity is not yet complete. While the Constitution separates the executive, legislative, and judicial powers, it does not in every instance vest these separate powers in completely separated agencies. Thus the Constitution says: "All legislative Powers herein granted shall be vested in a Congress of the United States," but in that same Article I the Constitution also says: "Every Bill which shall have passed the House of Representatives and the Senate, shall, before it become a Law, be presented to the President of the United States" for either his approval or disapproval, and, in the event of his disapproval, two-thirds of each House must agree to pass the bill notwithstanding the President's objections in order for it to become law. Just as the Constitution makes the President a partner in the legislative process, it makes one House of the Congress, the Senate, a partner in the executive process. Thus the Constitution says: "The executive Power shall be vested in a President of the United States of America," but in that same Article II it also requires the President to obtain the advice and consent of two-thirds of the Senators to make a treaty and of a majority of the Senators for the confirmation of appointments.

As I have indicated, the difficulty of defining the nature of the Presidency is heightened by the fact that the task is often undertaken at a time when two or sometimes all three branches of government are at loggerheads; one charging the other with usurpation of power and each regarding the other with suspicion, jealousy, and even fear. In this connection, I happen to be one of those who hold to the view that it is vitally necessary to strengthen the Congress so that it can meet the demands which changes in national and world society impose on it. I had a minor part as a consultant in the preparation of the report of the National Planning Association by Mr. Robert Heller, *Strengthening the Congress.*[12] Most of the recommendations in that report have my endorsement, just as many of the provisions of the Legislative Reorganization Act of 1946 seem to me to be steps in the right direction.

But it is important to draw a sharp line between "strengthening the Congress" in order that *as the Congress* it can do its work effectively and efficiently, and strengthening it at the expense of either the Presidency or the Courts. I endorse the first effort; I reject the second one. All branches of government need "strengthening" in terms of *themselves* and not at the expense of other branches of government, if they are to perform their duties, meet their obligations, and exercise their powers so as best to serve the people. I accept as a basic assumption in this presentation the separation of powers and the Constitutional assignment of duties and obligations among the institutions set up by the Constitution. This is not to say that I am setting myself up as an authority on the interpretation of that document. All I mean to say at this point is that I intend to avoid the frequent pitfalls of the "either-or" kind of judgments; that it must be the *Presidency* that should be strengthened and *nothing else;* or the *Congress* and *nothing else;* or the *Supreme Court* and *nothing else.* I shall continue to speak in this presentation of the Presidency as an institution in itself.

When one considers the historic ups and downs of the Presidency and its variations manifested in the personalities of the men who occupied it, one notices as an extremely interesting fact that the Presidency not only retains but continues to grow in prestige. Every President of the United States, with but one ex-

---

[12] *Strengthening the Congress,* by Robert Heller. Washington: National Planning Association, 1945.

ception, when he has been in office has been denounced as a despot, as a tyrant, as a dictator, as one who was using the power of the government to further his own personal ends and to achieve his own personal ambitions. The only President who was not so denounced was William Henry Harrison: he lived only one month after he was inaugurated. And yet in retrospect, if we look back over the list we see that we have had some strong Presidents and we have had some weak ones. But we have never had a bad one in the sense that he attempted to use the power of his office for personal aggrandizement; none who attempted to use the Army and Navy to seize permanent power, none who did not admit and freely adhere to all of the Constitutional limitations with respect to the term of office, election procedure, and all the rest of it.

The Presidency is by common consent the highest place among Americans, and it is by virtue of our peculiar Constitutional structure the highest political place held by any individual in the world. In the realm of social invention, this institution of the Presidency is perhaps the greatest contribution we have made. Here, at home, the existence of the Presidency molds the ambitions of countless millions of men. In their daydreams, millions of young American boys find themselves on the highroad to that great office; and now, in these days, all unsuspected, I do not doubt that an equal number of young American girls daydream of being the first woman Chief Executive.

Among mature men, the existence of the Presidency more directly governs their behavior. The political leader who, through an accident of birth in a foreign land, cannot be President, will behave quite differently from one who was born here in America and thus faces no Constitutional bar to the Presidency. The desire to be President exists on all sides. Lincoln called it a "grub" that once having got under a man's skin never left him. A man once stung by the Presidential bee, unlikely as his chances for the White House may seem to his neighbors, never recovers in this life. The Congress, for instance, may boast of its "dominance" over the Presidency, and yet the attraction of that office was vouched for only the other day by Senator Robert Taft, when he complained that the trouble with the 80th Congress was that every Republican in both Houses was a candidate for President. Nor has even the austere aloofness of the Supreme Court always been enough to keep the Presidential bee away from the ermine.

The remarkable aspect of the institution we have invented is not its prestige or power alone, but the fact that we have vested it with those attributes, without in the slightest degree relinquishing or relaxing our essential control over it. The complexities of the office we created are not carried in mind by every American at all times, any more than they are by the President in the White House. To the individual American, all Presidents are held to a high standard of behavior. When an incumbent fails to live up to what is expected of him, we place the blame upon the person and not upon the institution; and in reverse order, when the incumbent lives up to expectations, his successes are attributed to the institution and not the person. In a word, the Presidency has become the symbol in which the American people see made one their purpose, their plans, and their aspirations; the President has become the supreme servant who is expected to take the lead in realizing that purpose, those plans and aspirations.

The decision to vest all this power in one man came only after considerable debate in the Constitutional Convention. A respectable minority—respectable both in number and in the quality of persons who composed it—thought it safer to have a plural executive, usually spoken of in terms of three men. Some of the states at that time had a plural executive of three persons. Many of the states had a Governor whose executive acts were subject to the advice and consent of a Governor's council, and traces of this system persist in New England and North Carolina to this day. Nor was this issue closed with the adoption of the Constitution. Thomas Jefferson, who was in France at the time of the Constitutional Convention, was not fully satisfied for some years after the Constitution was in effect that the choice of a unitary executive was a right one. He was not opposed to a strong executive; on the contrary, he demanded it. But he was fearful of the ambitious man, and he suspected his great rival, Alexander Hamilton, of concealed monarchical inclinations. In 1800, the year before he himself became President, Jefferson wrote: [13]

... The republican world has long been looking with anxiety on the two experiments going on of a *single* elective Executive here, and a plurality there [in France]. Opinions have been considerably divided on the event in both countries. The greater opinion there has seemed to be heretofore in favor of a plurality, here it has been very generally, though not universally, in favor of a single elective Executive.

It was not long after that was written that Napoleon upset the French system and in all probability changed Jefferson's mind. At any rate, after 1801, when Jefferson himself became President, he said no more in favor of a plural executive.

But after Jefferson's day, in the early nineteenth century, numerous proposals for a plural executive in the United States continued to be put forward. Perhaps the last one advocated by any statesman of standing was the scheme proposed by John C. Calhoun. To preserve the Union and at the same time safeguard sectional interests, Calhoun proposed two Presidents, one from the North and one from the South. That proposal was rejected by what might paradoxically be called the acclamation of silence.

In contemporary times, critical recommendations for changes

[13] *The Writings of Thomas Jefferson.* New York: Derby & Jackson, Washington ed., 1859, Vol. IV, p. 315 f.

in the nature of the executive are forthcoming from those who would abolish the separation of the branches of government and reconstitute our government on the basis of Britain's parliamentary model. But these suggestions have not been taken seriously by either politicians or statesmen or by the people as a whole.

The executive power remains vested in the President. The Presidency is the symbol of national unity. Its personification in one man is by no means a symbol of one-man rule, one-man power, or one-man anything. It is rather that the people thus concentrate in a formally chosen leader their own responsibility for democratic rule.

The President does not obtain his executive power from an Act of Congress; nor is he responsible to the Congress or to the Supreme Court. The President holds his executive power by a direct mandate of the people as set forth in the Constitution, and it is toward the people as a whole—and not the Congress or the Supreme Court—that his lines of responsibility run.

Nor must it be supposed that his office was a gradual growth or an accommodation of compromises in the distribution of the powers of an existing office. The powers of the King and of the colonial Governors had been too long in abeyance, and, indeed, never had been applied on a continental scale when in 1787 this investiture by the people of executive power in the President was decreed. The idea of continuity with the past, which doubtless bulked large in the minds of the members of the Convention, may have been evidenced indirectly in the retention of the existing executive departments of Foreign Affairs, Treasury, War, and Post Office, as well as that of the Attorney General. But all of those posts were soon buried under the unitary creation of the Presidential office.

The Presidential office has, of course, grown tremendously, but it has grown in response to the demands made upon it by the people, who have increased in numbers and who have multiplied many times over their demands upon the services of government. These demands seek expression in the enactment of laws by the legislature and in the administration and execution of those laws by the Presidency. As I have just said, the President is directly responsible to the people, and, on the other hand, the people are directly responsible for the President. The principal features of that mutual responsibility will be examined in the lectures that follow.

The President: How We Choose Him

BEFORE THE Constitutional Convention invented the Electoral College as a means of choosing a President, a very strong sentiment existed in that body for the election of the President by the Congress. There is no need here to review that well-known story. Suffice it to say that the opposition to the election of the Executive by the legislature was based on several considerations. First, there was the then prevailing fear of "the tyranny of the legislature," which had burgeoned in the states since the surrender at Yorktown when there was neither executive nor judicial restraint upon the legislature, a circumstance which centered the opposition of all dissidents and minorities upon the legislature itself. Second, it was argued that the compound character of the proposed national legislature—one house to be representative of the people directly and of the states in proportion to their population, with the other to be representative of the states directly on a basis of equality—would make the choice of the President by the Congress a disjointed and awkward affair. Finally, it was argued that the election of the President by the Congress would do violence to the principle of the separation of powers among the three branches of government.

This difficulty was settled in a characteristically American way by a new invention: the Electoral College. The choice of the President was to be assigned to a special body in which each state would have a number of votes equal to the total number of its representatives in both Houses of the Congress; the members of the body to be chosen in each state in any manner that the legislature of that state might determine. It seems to have been expected that these electors, conscious of their high office but each acting in accordance with his own independent judgment, would consider which two men were best fitted to be President and then cast votes for these two men. When the votes were collected and canvassed by the Congress, the man who had a majority of all the votes would be President: the one who had the next highest number would be Vice President. If none had a majority, the House of Representatives would choose the President from amongst the three having the greatest number of electoral votes, with a similar reservation to the Senate of the choice of Vice President between the two having the greatest number of votes.

To the extent that the plan was devised to prevent the rise of "factions"—a word then usually applied in a derogatory manner to political parties—it was a complete failure. In the very first election, the electors unquestionably reflected the opinion of the country when every one of them cast one of his votes for George Washington, who was obviously destined to be the first President. There was no division into parties. The votes for second choice were well scattered, but 34 of them went to John Adams as against 35 for all others, and so Adams became the first Vice President. Nobody went to a polling place anywhere and voted for Washington or for electors who were pledged to vote for him. The electors were appointed by the legislatures of the states, except that the New York legislature failed to choose any at all. North Carolina and Rhode Island had not then ratified the Constitution, and so there were but 69 electors in all from ten states.

The factionalism that was to be avoided through the device of the Electoral College began to show up in bolder detail in the second election—though it was still confined to the choice of the

Vice President. While every elector voted for Washington, the second choices were divided on a factional basis, 77 votes going to John Adams, the Federalist, and 55 votes to an anti-Federalist choice, George Clinton getting 50, Thomas Jefferson 4, and Aaron Burr one. Adams, by virtue of his 77 votes as a Federalist, was reelected Vice President.

In the third election, party alignments showed up still more clearly. The Federalist John Adams got 71 votes and was elected President, and Thomas Jefferson, the Democratic-Republican, was elected Vice President with 68 votes. Even then there were no fewer than 48 scattered votes, showing that party discipline was not yet rigidly effective.

In the fourth election the party line-up was found to be all but perfect—indeed too perfect—under the system by which each elector voted for two men for President; for every Democratic-Republican elector without exception voted for both Thomas Jefferson and Aaron Burr, so that each got 73 votes. Every Federalist elector voted for John Adams, who got 65 votes, C. C. Pinckney got 64 votes, and one vote went to John Jay. The tie vote between Jefferson and Burr threw the election of the President into the House of Representatives where the vote, taken by states, was 10 for Jefferson, 4 for Burr, and 2 not cast.

These circumstances brought about the only Constitutional change we have made in the method of choosing the President. Nobody wanted anything like the Jefferson-Burr contest to happen again. Accordingly, the Twelfth Amendment was submitted in 1803, and on ratification became a part of the Constitution by September, 1804. The terms of this amendment preserved the institution of the Electoral College, and did not disturb the manner in which the electors were to be chosen; but it provided that the electors were to vote specifically for a President and a Vice President, one of whom at least should not be an inhabitant of the same state as themselves.

So by the fifth election the present Constitutional arrangement was perfected, but at the same time there began to emerge a non-Constitutional instrument for choosing a President which was destined in the end to overshadow completely the strictly Constitutional arrangement. Since that time, while the electors still enjoy a legal right to vote for whomsoever they please—indeed, in 1944, the Texas electors threatened to exercise this right—the essence of the choice of a President has passed from the electors to the political parties. Thereafter no elector, with the possible exception of one who refused to vote for Monroe in 1820 in order that Washington might still have the distinction of being the only unanimous choice, ever has failed to cast his vote in the Electoral College for his party candidate.

At this time, however, the parties themselves had no standard procedure for selecting their candidates, and in the early stages of party development the area of choice almost got back into the Congress—where the Constitution-makers had decided it should not go—because it seemed to be most convenient to have the party candidate chosen by caucus of the party members in the Congress. The rise of "King Caucus" as a method of choosing party candidates coincided with the monopoly of political power which the Democratic-Republican Party came to enjoy after the fifth election. By 1820 the Federalist Party was extinct, and for the space of two Presidential elections the United States experienced a one-party, or as some would have it a no-party, system. Not only was the party leadership in such entire control that it could choose the candidate to be blessed by the Congressional caucus, but that candidate invariably was the Secretary of State in the Cabinet of the previous President, and it seemed for a time that what was called the "Presidential succession" had been set up on a permanent basis.

In 1824 there was nominally but one party, the Democratic-Republican; it was, however, developing factionalism within itself, and it turned up with a multiplicity of Presidential aspirants. The revolt against the rule of King Caucus, against the so-called Presidential succession, was gaining great support. King Caucus gave his blessing to William H. Crawford of Georgia, but the state legislatures—and even county governments—began to make nominations, and there was no scheme for resolving these intraparty differences so that electors could vote for a single party candidate. In the end, Andrew Jackson emerged with the greatest number of votes, 99, followed by John Quincy Adams with 84, Crawford with 41, and Clay with 37. While John C. Calhoun had been elected Vice President by a clear majority, no one had a majority for President, and the Presidential election went into the House of Representatives where each state delegation had one vote. As the voting in the House was confined to the three highest names, Clay was dropped and John Quincy Adams chosen by the vote of 13 states, as against 7 for Jackson and 4 for Crawford. John Quincy Adams thus became the first minority President, and indeed the only one ever chosen who was second in electoral votes. In the storm that followed, the one-party or no-party system disappeared, the Democratic-Republican Party became the Democratic Party, with Jackson its undisputed leader, while the opposition under Adams and Clay took the name of National Republican, shortly to be changed to Whig.

This intensification of party feeling was accompanied by an insistence upon popular election of the Presidential electors, so that after 1828 they were chosen by popular vote within the states at the polls, except in South Carolina, where the electors continued to be appointed by the legislature until after 1860. The parties still lacked machinery for enforcing discipline on a national scale, and still there were occasional dissidents on either a local or even a state-wide basis. However, the Congressional caucus had disappeared and never again were the members of

Congress as such to choose the party candidates. The nominations came to be made in a very curious way: the County Courts began to nominate the President. I think Jackson was nominated by Blount County, Tennessee. Then the state legislatures began to make nominations; there was therefore no clear-cut choice, and there appeared a multiplicity of candidates from a single party for whom the electors would vote.

Again American resourcefulness brought forth an invention—the national party convention—which until this day is the means by which we choose the party candidates for President and thereby narrow the field of choice presented to the people at the polls. The national party convention has no Constitutional or statutory basis, yet it has become an immutable part of the American way. It has been criticized, of course. Just recently Mr. Roscoe Drummond of the *Christian Science Monitor* has brought forth a proposal for a national Presidential primary; but I doubt if he gave sufficient thought to the difficulties that would have to be overcome if his scheme is to be realized.

Curiously enough, the invention of the national party convention came not from one of the great parties but from a third party. The Anti-Masonic Party called a national convention to meet in Harrisburg, Pennsylvania, in 1831 and there nominated its candidates: William Wirt for President, and Amos Ellmaker for Vice President. They carried only two states and got only seven votes in the election of 1832. Nevertheless, it was this Anti-Masonic Party, which promptly vanished from the scene leaving but the vaguest memories behind it, which first introduced the method of choosing a President that Americans as a whole were soon to adopt and which they still employ.

John Quincy Adams was the last of the Presidents who had seemed to earn the high office by conspicuous service in the national government. After Washington, the captain of the Revolution itself, had come Adams, who had been Vice President, then Jefferson who had been Secretary of State under Washington and Vice President under Adams, and then Madison, Monroe, and John Quincy Adams, each of whom had served as Secretary of State throughout the administration of his predecessor.

The advent of Jackson marked a revolutionary change. He was a man not in the old manner, nor in the grand manner, and he was at once the cause and the effect of an ultrademocratic movement having its origin perhaps in the then West, but sweeping into the growing urban communities of the Atlantic seaboard where the industrial revolution was making itself felt. Even in the late nineteenth century Henry Adams [1] could with distaste and disdain call this a "grotesque alliance" of farmers with city day-laborers which upset the earlier aristocratic American notions—whether those of New England or of Virginia— about how to choose a President and the order of succession. Under Jackson there was no squeamishness about party or partisanship. Old Hickory was the Chief of Party as well as the Chief of State and he had no qualms about dictating the choice of his successor.

That successor, Martin Van Buren, was the first successful nominee of a party convention to gain the Presidency. Nominated and elected in 1836, renominated and defeated in 1840, Van Buren was himself deprived by the convention of 1844 of a third nomination and the chance of a second term by the "two-thirds rule"—a further invention to insure party discipline. Because of this rule, Van Buren was set aside at the Baltimore convention in 1844 and James K. Polk was put in. A great many people have referred to that event as a defeat for Jackson. I have never been quite in agreement with this view, for I once read in the *Nashville Banner,* issued on the day that Polk was nomi-

---

[1] *The Education of Henry Adams: An Autobiography.* Boston: Houghton Mifflin Co., 1918, p. 344.

nated, a report of an interview with Mr. Jackson in which he predicted to the editor that Mr. Polk would be the nominee. The first message ever sent over the telegraph was, it is true, the message announcing the nomination of Polk. But the telegraph existed only between Baltimore and Washington, so the extension of the news that day to Jackson in distant Nashville must have been by telepathy, or, as seems more likely, "Old Hickory" had some foreknowledge of what the upshot would be.

By 1840 the conventions, the type of party machinery, and the style of Presidential campaigns assumed the very characteristics that have persisted for more than a century and which to us now seem to be in all but minor details permanent and unchangeable.

The Whig convention of 1840, which named General William Henry Harrison, a military hero, for President and gave the second place on the ticket to John Tyler, a dissident anti-Van Buren Democrat, whooped it up for "Tippecanoe and Tyler too," and launched a campaign of hullabaloo, log cabins, and hard cider that swept the country in a fashion that no modern propagandist, press agent, or public relations counsellor ever has been able to surpass. And it was the Whig campaign song of 1840 that furnished the basis for the exaggerated importance that has since been given to the news of the September elections in Maine:

> And have you heard the news from Maine?
> And what old Maine did do?
>   How she went,
>   Hell bent,
>   For Governor Kent,
> And Tippecanoe and Tyler too.

As a matter of fact it was that very Whig victory of 1840 that prompted a Democratic President and a Democratic Congress, as soon as the Democrats got back into power in 1845, to exercise the Constitutional right of the Congress to fix a uniform day for choosing Presidential electors throughout the nation. That act was passed in 1845 and since that time the members of the Electoral College have been chosen on the first Tuesday after the first Monday in each Presidential election year. In South Carolina, however, the electors were chosen not by the people but by the state legislature until 1860.

It has been suspected that the reason the State of Maine continues to have its Congressional elections in September when all the other 47 states have synchronized them with the federal law which now requires the election of Presidential electors in November, is that because of this supposed importance of the news from Maine both the Democratic and Republican state committees have been able to extract a greater number of dollars from their respective national committees than otherwise might be possible. Whether the Gallup Poll is a serious threat to the classic event of the September Maine Congressional elections remains to be seen.

After Van Buren there ensued a long period of decline in the prestige of the Presidential office, a period of four or five decades in which, except during Lincoln's term of office, the Presidential power appeared to be withering away from the lack of vigor in its exercise or was being taken over by the Congress. Thus it was that in 1885 the youthful Woodrow Wilson could attribute the decline of the Presidency in large part to the convention system. In his *Congressional Government* he said:[2]

... After independence of choice on the part of the presidential electors had given place to the choice of presidential candidates by party conventions, it became absolutely necessary, in the eyes of politicians, and more and more necessary as time went on, to make expediency and availability the only rules of selection. As each party, when in convention assembled, spoke only those opinions which seemed to have received the sanction of the general voice, carefully

[2] *Congressional Government: A Study in American Politics,* by Woodrow Wilson. Boston: Houghton Mifflin Co., 15th ed., 1900, p. 42 ff.

suppressing in its "platform" all unpopular political tenets, and scrupulously omitting mention of every doctrine that might be looked upon as characteristic and as part of a peculiar and original programme, so, when the presidential candidate came to be chosen, it was recognized as imperatively necessary that he should have as short a political record as possible, and that he should wear a clean and irreproachable insignificance. "Gentlemen," said a distinguished American public man, "I would make an excellent President, but a very poor candidate." A decisive career which gives a man a well-understood place in public estimation constitutes a positive disability for the presidency; because candidacy must precede election, and the shoals of candidacy can be passed only by a light boat which carries little freight and can be turned readily about to suit the intricacies of the passage.

So wrote Woodrow Wilson at twenty-nine. However, in 1900, in writing a new introduction to the same book, after Presidential power had been so vigorously exercised by Grover Cleveland and after the prestige of the Presidency had been restored and revived by the events of the War with Spain, and when Mr. McKinley was on the eve of reelection, the maturing Woodrow Wilson proclaimed that he had changed his mind. In that preface he said: [3]

> Much the most important change to be noticed is the result of the war with Spain upon the lodgment and exercise of power within our federal system: the greatly increased power and opportunity for constructive statesmanship given the President, by the plunge into international politics and into the administration of distant dependencies, which has been that war's most striking and momentous consequence. . . . The President of the United States is now, as of course, at the front of affairs, as no president, except Lincoln, has been since the first quarter of the nineteenth century, when the foreign relations of the new nation had first to be adjusted. . . .
>
> . . . . . .
>
> It may be, too, that the new leadership of the Executive, inasmuch as it is likely to last, will have a very far-reaching effect upon our

---

[3] *Ibid.*, pp. xi-xiii, Preface to 15th edition.

whole method of government . . . . It may bring about, as a consequence, an integration which will substitute statesmanship for government by mass meeting. It may put this whole volume hopelessly out of date.

Nevertheless, much that Wilson said in his youthful essay still stands, for the conventions, representing the parties, seek the candidates who will have the greatest popular appeal in all parts of the country and therefore the greatest chance of garnering the most electoral votes. Of the eight Presidents I have seen in the White House since I first went to Washington as a newspaper correspondent, four had been Governors of states—Theodore Roosevelt, Woodrow Wilson, Calvin Coolidge, and Franklin D. Roosevelt; two had been members of the Senate—Warren G. Harding and Harry S. Truman; and two—William H. Taft and Herbert Hoover—had had experience in public administration under the national government.

Of these eight no fewer than three were not in the first instance chosen by a party convention to be President. Theodore Roosevelt, Calvin Coolidge, and Harry S. Truman were nominated for the office of Vice President, a choice which in the case of Theodore Roosevelt and Calvin Coolidge was ratified by a party nomination for another term and approved by the people at the polls. Of the other five, only two won in a hot interparty political fight after "slugging it out" with powerful contenders—Woodrow Wilson and Franklin D. Roosevelt.

A good many stories are afloat about Woodrow Wilson and his nomination by the Democratic national convention at Baltimore in 1912. Some of these stories have been deemed to be contradictory of the others, but in my opinion all of them are substantially true. For example, Mr. McAdoo, who was to become Secretary of the Treasury, has told his tale of the happenings; Mr. Tumulty, who was to become President Wilson's secretary, has told his; Mr. McCombs, who was the Wilson campaign manager at the convention, has told his; others have told theirs; and now, if I may, I shall tell mine.

The core of truth in all these accounts is simply that Wilson won first Bryan and then the convention by conspicuous courage in taking the side of the progressive wing of the party and by his dogged determination to fight the fight to a finish.

When that convention assembled, the two principal contenders for the nomination were the Speaker of the House of Representatives, Champ Clark, and the Governor of New Jersey, Woodrow Wilson. Neither had a majority of the delegates, much less the two-thirds required for the nomination. The struggle between the two men was, however, eclipsed at the very start by the fight between the two wings of the party precipitated by William Jennings Bryan in a telegram addressed to all the aspirants, favorite sons included, demanding that the convention choose a Progressive (with a capital "P") and not a reactionary for its temporary chairman. To Mr. Bryan's telegram Governor Wilson replied, "You are quite right." All the others took evasive action. And that determined the line-up.

The Bryan candidate for temporary chairman was defeated, but that very defeat and the defeat of other Bryan moves gave the three-time nominee again and again the opportunity to cast his oratorical spell over the convention, to rally his "progressive" following, to undermine the influence of those whom he called "the reactionaries."

On the third day, and the ninth ballot (I think it was), Clark, who had led in the voting from the first, got a majority of the votes. On the next ballot, however, the expected break in the Wilson lines failed to materialize, and Clark gained but two. Despite the fact that the two-thirds rule had prevailed in Democratic conventions from 1844, no man who had once got a majority ever had failed to get the necessary additional votes to give him two-thirds of the votes.

The Wilson campaign headquarters were in the Emerson Hotel. As the majority went to Clark for the second time, Mr. McCombs told me to hurry to the hotel and get one of the Governor's secretaries on the telephone and to keep him on until he, McCombs, could get there. Long-distance telephoning was not quite so easy nor so sure in those days, and such precautions were not infrequent.

There was plenty of time for Mr. McCombs to have sent a telegram advising Governor Wilson to withdraw; plenty of time for Mr. Tumulty to have torn that telegram to bits, as he says he did. There was plenty of time for Mr. McCombs to have telephoned the Governor from the Convention Hall and for him to have made the report of that conversation to Mr. McAdoo, as Mr. McAdoo says he did. There was plenty of time for all those things to have happened in the half-hour before Mr. McCombs got to the hotel room.

Over the telephone I had reached Walter Measday, one of the Governor's secretaries at Sea Girt, the summer home of the Governor of New Jersey. I told him what had happened, and that McCombs was in a panic and was trying to reach the Governor to advise him to withdraw. I also told him that I thought there was no reason to withdraw—that I doubted whether Clark ever would have got a majority had it not been for the protection of the two-thirds rule. I was sure that Mr. Bryan, who as a delegate from Nebraska instructed for Clark, still obeying his mandate, would have broken away if a majority had meant nomination—and, of course, there was more talk of the same sort all carried on in tense excitement.

Then into the hotel room came McCombs, with McAdoo almost on his heels. "Get the Governor on the wire," said McCombs, who was pale and shaky in the face of what he assumed to be defeat. "Mac," (to McAdoo) "he must withdraw." "He must not," shouted McAdoo, and then in came

Charles W. Bryan, the brother of the Peerless Leader, Senator John W. Kern of Indiana, and Senator Luke Lea of Tennessee— all of whom were against Clark, but probably hoped that the deadlock would produce a fourth nomination for Bryan, a hope I believe Bryan himself did not then share.

I heard the Governor's voice on the telephone. "Governor," I said, "this is Brownlow. Mr. McCombs wishes to speak to you."

McCombs was a very slight man, not strong at any time and now in a veritable palsy of fear. McAdoo was very tall, very strong, very sure of himself. With one sweep of his forearm McAdoo brushed McCombs to one side and seized the telephone. "Governor," he said, "McCombs is going to beg you to withdraw. I ask you not to. He is the only one of your friends who is afraid." Then he handed the telephone receiver to the agitated McCombs. We listened to McCombs plead with Mr. Wilson to recognize the fact of the majority vote for Clark, to save the party, to avoid the danger of a split, and so on. There was a brief moment of silence and McCombs handed the phone to me. I heard a voice. It was Woodrow Wilson's. What it said was this:

"May I suggest that you tell my friends of the press that I shall not withdraw."

Never have I left a place in a greater hurry. That was on Friday. Even the next day McCombs persisted in his efforts, and at one time gave McAdoo the impression that the Governor had begun also to weaken. But there was no break. The roll calls went on and the shouting. It was not until the next Tuesday and on the forty-third ballot that the necessary two-thirds voted for Wilson.

In contrast with Wilson, Senator Harding was a dark horse— the choice of party leaders—when the Republican convention of 1920 for a long time had been unable to decide among the rival candidacies of Governor Frank O. Lowden and General Leonard D. Wood, who had tested their popularity in pre-election campaigns. This choice was made not in the clamor of an open fight on the convention floor, as in Wilson's case, but in the hushed quiet of a smoke-filled room.

Mr. Taft and Mr. Hoover, were chosen apparently because of their distinguished records as successful administrators. Neither was accounted to be primarily a politician. Mr. Taft had indeed been a circuit judge, but his services as Solicitor General, as our Proconsul in the Philippines, and as Secretary of War commended him not only to his predecessor, Theodore Roosevelt, who as supreme party leader gave him the nod, but also to the people and presumably to the delegates at the convention. He was hailed as "the best equipped and best trained man ever to become President." The next Republican national convention renominated him, but his lieutenants were forced to use the steam roller to accomplish their purpose; the party split in two; Roosevelt led the Bull Moose revolt; and Taft came out in the election with only two states, Vermont and Utah, and only eight votes in the Electoral College. Mr. Hoover, an engineer who had demonstrated his great administrative capacity as Food Administrator during the war, as Relief Commissioner to stricken Europe, and in eight years' brilliant work as Secretary of Commerce, also was chosen because of his training and equipment and not because he was primarily a politician. His party convention renominated him, but he also was doomed to defeat. Of the Presidents I have named, Mr. Taft and Mr. Hoover were the only ones who were not primarily party politicians, and neither had any zest for the political part of the job of President. Neither liked to play the game. All of the others—Theodore Roosevelt, Wilson, Harding, Coolidge, Franklin D. Roosevelt— I suspect, enjoyed that particular game more than any other; and of Mr. Truman it may be said that there is no substantial evidence that it is distasteful to him.

The terms of these eight Presidents have spread over twelve Presidential elections, and in only two of them has there been a third party large enough to capture an electoral vote, the Bull Moose Progressive Party in 1912, which carried six states, and the La Follette Progressive Party in 1924, which carried only Wisconsin. With these exceptions, we may say that we operate under a two-party system and therefore one of the candidates chosen by one of the major party conventions is bound to be defeated. Taking the same period, the catalogue of the defeated candidates is a little longer. When in 1904 I met Mr. Theodore Roosevelt in the White House, he was serving out the term for which McKinley and he had defeated the Democratic ticket of Bryan and Stevenson. Then, among other defeated candidates, there followed Alton B. Parker, Mr. Bryan again, Taft and Theodore Roosevelt in 1912, Charles E. Hughes, James M. Cox, John W. Davis, Alfred E. Smith, Herbert Hoover, Alfred M. Landon, Wendell Willkie, and Thomas E. Dewey.

Of these national convention choices fated for defeat, three already had served as President—Taft, Theodore Roosevelt, and Hoover. Parker had been a judge, as also had Hughes; but Hughes, Cox, Smith, Landon, and Dewey—no fewer than five —had been Governors of their states. Only Davis had had a public career which combined the administrative and the legislative, as Solicitor General and as a member of Congress, and he had been the dark horse compromise after the Democratic convention of 1924 had been unable to resolve the deadlock between Smith and McAdoo, the two preconvention favorites. The other two defeated candidates were Bryan, whose brief service in Congress was all but forgotten, and Willkie, who was without previous political experience.

In all this list of defeated candidates, excluding the three who already had served as President, it is hard to find more than three who were looked upon by their fellows as primarily politicians with a genuine flair for playing the great game. They were Bryan, Smith, and Dewey. Certainly party politics was not a matter of prime priority in the minds of Governor Hughes, Governor Cox, Governor Landon, or Mr. Davis, although all of them had exhibited considerable skill when drafted as players. The greatest politician of them all was Bryan. Willkie was an amateur, but one who showed much promise, and had it not been for his untimely death perhaps he would have made the top grade amongst the professionals.

Party conventions being what they are, grand national constituent assemblies of politicians devoted to partisan political purposes, interested in winning, and naturally sympathetic to persons who are likewise politicians, it is worth while I think to inquire into at least some of the general considerations which seem to have determined their choices—for their choices under the prevailing system inevitably narrow the choice of the people for the Presidency to that between two partisan candidates.

Every one of these men was chosen on the basis of what was deemed to be at the moment his superior "availability." It must not be imagined that the word "availability" used with this special meaning indicates that these men were the only ones who were available in the sense that they would accept the nomination. There is never any doubt of "availability" in that sense. What the party counsellors mean when they use the word is that they believe, when all is said and done, this is the particular man who will be most able to hold together the factions, cliques, and sectional and other divergent groups within the party, that at the same time he will have the greatest appeal both for the votes of those independents who are committed to neither party and of the dissidents in the other party who may revolt against the nominee of their own convention, and that therefore he is the most "available."

Sometimes this availability is determined as the result of

hurried consultation after an open battle in which two or more
leading candidates have killed each other off, as in the cases of
Harding and of Davis; sometimes it is the result of long months
or even years of canny calculation by the leading candidate and
his cohorts, as in the cases of Woodrow Wilson and Franklin D.
Roosevelt; and sometimes it is determined by a grim but necessarily more or less hushed struggle behind the scenes between
the leaders of the rival wings of the party—grim because of the
importance they attach to it, hushed because too forthright an
identification of their man with either wing would by definition
diminish his "availability," as was the case with Parker.

In any of these three contingencies of availability that I have
been discussing, or in any modifications of them, the politicians
are forced to take into account two elements not entirely within
their control. One is the tide of public opinion that may be
sweeping through the country; the other, the emotional ebulli-
tion within the cauldron of the convention itself. Occasionally
that cauldron boils over; the connivers wise and cunning alike
are swept aside, and the convention makes its own choice in a
clamorous outburst of feeling, as in the case of Bryan in 1896
and Willkie in 1940.

While such emotional storms are sometimes materially as-
sisted from the outside, as was certainly true in the case of Mr.
Willkie, Bryan whirled his own cyclone. Young, handsome, an
orator in possession of a carefully written and perfectly memorized speech, with perfect control of a truly marvelous voice, he
stood on the very spot now occupied by the silver screen in the
Tower Theatre in Chicago, just across the University of Chicago
campus, and in a few minutes won fame and party leadership
and put his name on the long roster of those who sought, but
vainly, the prize of the Presidency.

In the sign of the Crown of Thorns and the Cross of Gold,
Bryan assumed in that one speech the leadership of his party in

the interest of one wing of that party and in bold defiance of its conservative faction, which then was represented and led by the President of the United States, Grover Cleveland.

That a forthright factional stand will stir a convention to a frenzy was again exemplified in Chicago sixteen years later, when Theodore Roosevelt, defying the conservative wing of his party and its representative, the then President of the United States, William Howard Taft, called on the Bull Moose to stand at Armageddon and battle for the Lord.

Mr. Bryan's performance was perhaps the most remarkable individual feat in the history of conventions, for he remained the dominant figure in five successive Democratic national conventions. In 1896 and 1900 he was himself the nominee. In 1904 the votes went to the candidate of the conservative wing, Judge Parker; but Mr. Bryan in person was the center of the convention itself, and despite his lack of control of its voting he managed to keep such a hold on his party leadership that he resumed it without question on the morning after Parker met his inevitable defeat. In 1908 Mr. Bryan again nominated himself. Then, in 1912, by personal domination of the convention he nominated Woodrow Wilson and defeated Champ Clark.

Just a little while before that, Mr. Wilson had been writing letters to Mr. Adrian H. Joline in Kansas saying: "I wish we could knock Mr. Bryan into a cocked hat, once and for all." That was embarrassing, but Mr. Wilson, despite what was said about him in later years, had his flexible side; he was not composed entirely of Presbyterian granite; he could yield when necessary. He did persuade Mr. Bryan to support him for President, and then rewarded him in the characteristic and normal political manner by making him the head of the Cabinet. But from the day Bryan went into the Cabinet as Secretary of State he was no longer the leader of the Democratic Party. Mr. Wilson took over that job.

National conventions are not only arenas in which personal and organizational rivalries are fought out (rivalries among leaders, bosses, machines, and pressure groups); they are not only the proving grounds in which ambitious candidates seek their chance to be placed before the electorate as contenders for the supreme prize of the Presidency: national conventions are also assemblies of party delegates who differ in their opinions about measures as well as men, and who struggle to control the convention, its platform, and its choice of a nominee in the interest of their particular convictions and predilections.

Each of the parties has two rival wings and in turn these rival wings are cut across by lines of sectional and other special interests. It is difficult in any universally satisfactory manner even to give names to these wings. Perhaps they may be identified as Conservative and Liberal, or loosely, in modern terminology, as Right and Left. Rarely would these labels have been accepted by the people concerned, and frequently what is a label today becomes an epithet tomorrow.

From the time when the party convention was invented we have used dozens of pairs of labels to denominate party factions; although sometimes these very same names are also used to describe the principal rival parties themselves. Thus sometimes the names may simply be taken from prevailing issues, as Bank and Anti-Bank, Texas and Anti-Texas, Nebraska and Anti-Nebraska, Free Soil and Squatter Sovereignty. Sometimes they are curious contrivances, such as Barn Burners against Hunkers, and Locofoco against Tammany, Bull Moose against Standpatter.

Before the Civil War both the Whig and the Democratic parties had each its pro-slavery and its anti-slavery wing. After the Civil War the Republicans were divided for a time into Radicals and Conservatives, and then later into Radicals and Liberals; the Liberals and Conservatives, oddly enough, being the same group. In the period of my own observation since 1904, these rivalries have continued in each of the great parties. Each party had its Gold wing and its Silver wing. The Democrats were divided as between Bryanites and Anti-Bryanites; the Republicans as between Standpatters and Insurgents. Sometimes, whatever the labels or the epithets, the factions are pro-Business or anti-Big Business, pro-Labor or anti-Labor, one side saying that it puts men above money and the other side denying that it elevates money above men. And, of late, both parties have had their deep differences of opinion with respect to foreign affairs: some have been isolationists, some have been internationalists. And it is because these lines crisscross each other that we can still have a two-party system, two parties grouped around quite generalized traditions, two parties, neither of which is logically devoted to any doctrinaire ideology.

What the delegates to the convention want is to name a man who will win in the coming November and at the same time to get one who will incline slightly to the right or slightly to the left, as the individual delegate, or at any rate as the state delegation of which he is a member, is also inclined. The delegates also are anxious that this rivalry should not break into an open factional fight and thus minimize the chances of victory in the election. Therefore they are apt to select as Vice President a man from the wing of the party that has been defeated and disappointed in the major choice, and usually they leave the actual choice of the "running mate" to the man they have just named to lead the ticket.

In most cases this intraparty rivalry is hush-hushed as soon as the convention is over and the delegates go back home to try to organize for a winning campaign. But once in a while the difference of opinion is so great that the party splits, as did both Democrats and Republicans in 1896 on the silver issue, and as did the Republican Party in 1912 when the bolting Progressives actually gathered more votes at the polls than did the regular Republicans. For the most part, however, the Right wing is stronger than the Left in the Republican Party; the Left wing is stronger than the Right in the Democratic Party. The Democratic Party is more apt to select actual leaders as candidates than is the Republican, and certainly the Democrats are more persistent in sticking to their leaders as nominees.

In sixty years of conventions since 1884, the Democrats have nominated eight men for President, the Republicans twelve. No Republican ever has received more than two nominations, whereas in this period Mr. Cleveland was nominated three times, Mr. Bryan three times, and Franklin D. Roosevelt four times. In the case of both Cleveland and Bryan the Democrats did not hesitate again and again to nominate a candidate who theretofore had been defeated; the Republicans never have chosen a man who once had failed. It may be that Governor Dewey in 1948 will break this record. Good Guess!

National conventions are also subjected to great pressures through organized schemes to set an emotional current sweeping toward one or another candidate. This is nothing new. The nation may indeed owe one of its greatest debts of gratitude to the organized claque that here in Chicago in 1860, under the sign "Vox Populi, Vox Dei," so tipped the scales that Abraham Lincoln was nominated, rather than Seward. But these efforts to "organize" enthusiasm at conventions have sometimes backfired. At the Democratic convention of 1912 in Baltimore I felt quite sure that the local committee, which was for Champ Clark, made a terrible blunder when it decorated the whole town with Maryland flags. Not everybody in the other forty-seven states was familiar with Maryland's beautiful flag of orange and black, but every Princetonian who emerged from a railway station saw the Princeton colors and yelled, "The town is on fire for Wilson!"

It was in 1904 that I attended my first national convention. That was here in Chicago, too, in the building then called the Coliseum, at 18th Street on Michigan Avenue. It was a convention which met and was required by the dogged will of the people to nominate a man whom hardly anybody in the convention wanted. It was a convention of politicians. Most of them hated their President, Theodore Roosevelt. Most of them knew he was President because Mr. Platt, the Republican Boss of New York, in his too clever way in 1900 wanted to kick him out of the Governor's mansion in Albany and upstairs into the Vice Presidency. But McKinley was assassinated; Theodore Roosevelt became President, and now he must be nominated in his own right for the Presidency.

The convention did not like it a bit. It was cold, emotionless, and finally the President had to whip up spirit by sending a message by telegraph: "Pericardis alive or Raisuli dead," and all of us whooped it up for a war with the Barbary Pirates— a war that never came off. Pericardis, I should explain, was a naturalized American citizen of Greek birth who at that time was a prisoner of a Moroccan chieftain named Raisuli. The United States was demanding that he be freed, and that demand was used to put a little life into an all but dead national convention. Pericardis was released.

Beginning in 1924, when the death struggle between Smith and McAdoo in the Democratic convention filtered through thousands of pairs of headphones on thousands of homemade crystal radio sets, the convention walls no longer set the boundaries of the conventions. In Philadelphia in 1940 the claque in the galleries chanting "We want Willkie" thrilled millions of listeners from coast to coast, and though television was not yet available, the bouncing reaction was made manifest in hundreds of different ways on the convention floor.

An American invention but rarely imitated and never rivalled

in any other country, the national party convention may sometimes seem to the serious student of politics hardly fitted for its
high duty and grave responsibility. The national convention
was the apex of a political structure in which similar conventions in township, county, city, and state performed a similar
office in choosing the candidates for lesser positions. The local
conventions proved to be too easily swayed, whether by bun-
combe, booze, or boodle, with the consequence that a reform
movement all but abolished them and substituted the direct
primary. During the period when the primary reform was
riding to triumph in state and local party government, many
voices were raised in favor of a direct Presidential primary.
But here the very nature of the federal structure, the political
equality of the states, the selection of the Presidential electors
by states, as well as the practical difficulties of promoting personal candidatures in a general Presidential primary, stopped
the movement. In some states Presidential preference primaries
have been set up by law, but the most that they have done is to
influence the votes of the delegates from those particular states
in the initial stages of the convention balloting. For the past two
decades, unassailed and apparently unassailable, the national
party convention stands as the instrument through which we,
the American people, effect the choice of the President of the
United States.

Let it be understood that I do not make this statement in dep-
recation or derogation of the system. It may be irrational, it
is certainly noisy, it is occasionally disorderly, but on the whole
the test of time has shown that it is democratic. Furthermore,
the institution of the national convention, in my opinion, has
made a major contribution toward the conservation of one of
the most valuable and most fundamental political resources of
this nation, namely, the two-party system. The convention usually recognizes the necessity of party political skill as a pre-

requisite to its choice, and it invariably applies the test of availability. This means that it all but automatically rejects aspirants
for the Presidential nomination who are too intimately identified with a geographical section, an economic group, or a social
stratum. In the search to discover a candidate who can win, the
convention seeks for one who will hold together all the factions
within the party, north and south, east and west, rich and poor,
conservative and liberal, right and left; and when it has found
its man it mounts him on a platform which is a skillful compromise of promises to help every considerable group and of
warnings that the other party will not do so. By this operation
the doctrinaire ideologist is eliminated. The choice therefore is
apt to fall on one who seems to be tolerant enough to listen to
various views and flexible enough to become identified as the
leader of many causes; many causes not always contradictory in
substance but frequently rivals for priority in prestige.

Perfectionists may and do bemoan these things; may cry out
for a realignment of parties with all of the conservatives in one
and all of the liberals in the other; may bewail the fact that
under our system there is no such party discipline as is necessary
to the working of the parliamentary system; and may, as they
frequently do, see the way out by advocating a third party,
seemingly unconscious of the self-defeating implications of such
a move. But if one is too disgusted with some manifestation of
practical politics and is tempted to join these perfectionists, I
suggest that one should first make a laboratory test. It is quite
simple. Into a room invite twelve of your acquaintances who
think themselves conservatives, and twelve who think themselves liberals. Ask each for a definition of his own self-avowed
label, stir up a lively debate, and decant the result. It will be
twenty-four parties.

On the other hand, the doctrinaire ideological party in a federal republic of vast geographical extent, huge population, and

an almost infinitely varied assortment of economic and social groups would, even under the Presidential system, be a divisive influence and make for disunity. In France with its regime centralized after the destruction of the historic provinces of the *ancien régime,* without any check of federalism and without any strong executive, the logical doctrinaire devotion to ideologies has made for a plurality of parties and at the same time for paralysis of the national will. In England the two-party system has, on the whole, survived, each with its wings and factions, and there, in a centralized national government with the tradition of unity under a constitutional monarch, the parliamentary system has been notably successful; but it is a success, I am persuaded with Mr. Don K. Price,[4] which would not necessarily be repeated if the scheme were to be applied in a republican and a federal structure. Our parties, for all their flexibility, for all their shifting, for all their attempts to placate all shades of opinion within their ranks, still remain an effective means for bipolarizing the political opinion of the country. And for the very reason that they do maintain this flexibility, that bipolarity does not split the nation into two implacable factions.

Thus, every four years the national conventions narrow our choice for President to two men. Then the two men, each backed by his own party, wage the battle of the campaign for votes, using every possible device to influence and persuade the individual voter. Blandishment and imprecation, promise and denunciation—now there is no flexibility, now all is white or else all is black. Passions are engendered, men and women get angry, subscribers stop their newspapers, neighbors quit speaking to each other, boys fight and girls quarrel; public opinion polls are published, straw votes are taken, rallies are held, dem-

---

[4] "The Parliamentary and Presidential Systems," by Don K. Price, *Public Administration Review,* Vol. III, No. 4, Autumn 1943, pp. 317–34.

onstrations organized, until at the first of November it must seem to that mythical traveler from Mars that civil war is inevitable.

And on Tuesday night in front of the bulletin boards and around the radios everybody listens, until toward midnight or some time perhaps on Wednesday morning the great American people with one voice exclaims, "Well, that's that!" and settles back for another four years. Not everywhere are the results of elections taken so calmly.

In a partisan political fight we have chosen the candidate of one political party or the other to be our President. He will be inaugurated come January 20. And then, so curiously inconsistent are we (perhaps this is a reflection of that flexibility that I have been discussing) that we acclaim him President of all the people and then instantly develop a distaste for his doing anything that even smacks of the partisan. He may be, indeed he must be, still the leader of a political party, but for most of us he is not now primarily that: rather, he is the Chief of State, the Chief of Government, and the personified symbol of America.

In such fashion have we chosen Presidents—thus far, thirty-two of them. Actually of the thirty-two men who served as President, but twenty-five were chosen to be President, as seven of them were elected in the first instance to be Vice President —Tyler, Fillmore, Johnson, Arthur, Theodore Roosevelt, Coolidge, and Truman. Of these seven, two were later selected to be President in their own right—Theodore Roosevelt and Calvin Coolidge. In which of these categories history will place Harry Truman is for 1948 to discover.

Truly it may be said in this connection that "many are called, but few are chosen." The choice, in the large and at the end, is the choice of the people; but it is also true that in the first instance the man usually chooses himself. After that (at least so it has been for a full century) if he can persuade a national convention to ratify his own choice of himself, then his name is pitted against that of the nominees of the other national conventions and the people at the polls decide between the parties and their candidates. Even this process is yet carried on by states and is exercised through the machinery of the Electoral College.

It is not alone by reading the list of the twenty-five we have chosen to be President that we may understand the relationship of party and of personality, the influence of policy and ambition, on these choices. We should read also the longer, the much longer list of those who sought and did not find, who ran and did not win.

On that list, too, there loom great names whose luster still is bright, as well as lesser names now dimmed but which once seemed destined for eternal fame—Jay and Pinckney; Burr and Clinton; William H. Crawford and Hugh Lawsom White; Clay and Webster; Calhoun and Benton; Cass and Marcy; William H. Seward and Stephen A. Douglas; Greeley and Seymour; John Sherman; James G. Blaine; Samuel J. Tilden; Belva A. Lockwood and Ben Butler; Richard P. Bland and William Jennings Bryan; McAdoo and Davis; Frank O. Lowden and Leonard D. Wood; La Follette and Cox; Al Smith and Alf Landon; Wendell Willkie, and many, many more who once dreamed the dream and had good reason to believe that that dream might come true.

Some few of the twenty-five that were chosen to be President had not been themselves active candidates; several of the seven who first were selected as Vice Presidents were not. But most of them had the ambition and the courage to make the try. Nearly all of them were backed by political parties. Few of them were finally elected merely because of a party label; most of them won because at that time and in that day both the party and the candidate represented something that the most of the people believed that particular man could do for them that they wanted done.

One thing about the roll call is impressive. Just as Lincoln, the sixteenth President, said that on the whole all his forerunners had done a good job, so now it may be said that generally all the thirty-two have done well. Never has a bad man been elected. Some of them have been better than others, no doubt. Some of them have been stronger than others, it cannot be disputed. Some of the weak ones have been imposed upon by unworthy friends and associates. Some of them have been leaders and a few have been content rather to follow than to lead. But during the whole century and a half and more, during the whole history of the thirty-two Presidents, not one has been recreant to his high trust, a trust perhaps best expressed in what was at the very first proposed by General Washington as the title of the office: "His Highness, the President of the United States of America and the Protector of Their Liberties."

May I repeat: every President during his term of office has been denounced as a coward and a poltroon. Almost every one has been called a tyrant. Almost every one has been accused of trying to subvert the Constitution. But in the retrospect we see that none has used his power to aggrandize himself at the expense of our settled institutions; none has ruled by outright force—although Lincoln used force to prevent disunion. And none, once he is gone, is called Dictator.

Clumsy as it may sometimes seem to be, the way we choose our President nevertheless works out pretty well.

[III]

What We Expect the President to Do

WHATEVER ELSE A President newly come to the White House may look forward to, he will, if he be wise, realize from the first moment that he is certain to disappoint the hopes of many of the members of his constituency who collectively compose the nation. There are at least two reasons in support of this expectation. In the first place, as the President exercises the duties of his high office he will be compelled to make choices, and every choice he makes, whether in respect of measures or of men, will displease or disillusion those who do not agree with him. In the second place—and in the number of citizens affected this is the more important category—the nation expects more of the President than he can possibly do; more than we give him either the authority or the means to do. Thus, expecting from him the impossible, inevitably we shall be disappointed in his performance.

That is merely another way of saying that by custom and tradition as well as by statute and Constitution, we have endowed the Presidency with such lofty attributes that any man chosen by us to be the President, while he is charged with the obligation to aspire, may never quite achieve the full splendor of its lofty heights. That these things are true flows from the fact that we expect the President to symbolize the nation in his office and in his person. It follows, then, that each of us identifies the President with his own private and particular notion of what this nation is and what Americans are. Each person expects the President to mirror that image, and as no two of us have precisely the same idea of our national being and destiny, we are inevitably disturbed when the man who symbolizes them does not conform to our ideals.

It is precisely because we do so differ that we organize into groups in which these differences of outlook, opinion, and hopes seem smaller, and then by processes of political alchemy organize ourselves into two political parties. One of these parties —sometimes it is the one that puts forward the better candidate, sometimes it is the one with the better platform of promises or the better platform of protests—sees its choice for President become the nation's choice at the polls. The candidate becomes President. Just after he takes the oath of office, many of us— I am inclined to think most of us, perhaps indeed all of us except the few who are professional politicians—tend to forget that he was first a party choice and a party leader. More than that, we seem at this particular stage to regret the necessity for party machinery, and exhibit displeasure at any sign of partisan activity by the President.

At this stage we insist—and in deference to public opinion many Presidents at the commencement of their term of office have publicly proclaimed—that the President is not the President of a party but the President of all the people, as of course he is. Thus is created that phenomenon we call "the Presidential honeymoon." At first, everybody seems to be with the President; he seems to be the man we may count on to continue to do all the things that his predecessor did of which we approved, and upon whom we may rely to correct and redress all the errors made by his predecessor. Even the members of the opposition party (with the exception, perhaps, of the professionals) who proclaimed during the campaign his unfitness for the office, at this stage seem to say: "Well, after all, he's a good fellow. Let's back him up and give him a chance." His partisans, of course, hail him as one who will solve all problems.

As the honeymoon draws to its inevitable end, we no longer expect the President completely to fulfill our notions of what the symbol of the nation should be, but by the same token we tend to emphasize and insist upon our expectations that he will do for us certain specific things. We expect the President to be, first, a competent manager of the machinery of government; second, a skilled engineer of the economy of the nation; and, third, a faithful representative of the opinion of the people. These three expectations I have set down in the inverse order of their importance in popular esteem, but perhaps in their correct order with respect to the choices and decisions the President must make if he is to fulfill to the maximum what the citizens expect of him. Yet it must not be imagined for an instant that because we accept the new President as President of all the people and make manifest our distaste when he too patently shows that he is also party leader, that he can afford to abandon his party role. What is required of him if he is to be successful is that—he become not only the leader of the political party but the political leader of the country as well.

Woodrow Wilson stated this problem in a lecture he gave at Columbia University in 1907. This was four years before he became Governor of New Jersey and six years before he became President; at a time when he was regarded primarily as a professor and the president of Princeton; at a time when his political powers were for the most part unrecognized; and at a time when he was not *en rapport* with the leadership of his own party—for he was then writing to Mr. Adrian H. Joline the famous letter in which he expressed the wish that he might knock Mr. Bryan into a cocked hat. Speaking of the President of the United States as a political leader, Mr. Wilson said: [1]

---

[1] *Constitutional Government in the United States,* by Woodrow Wilson. New York: The Columbia University Press, 1908, p. 67 ff.

He cannot escape being the leader of his party except by incapacity and lack of personal force, because he is at once the choice of the party and of the nation. He is the party nominee, and the only party nominee for whom the whole nation votes. Members of the House and Senate are representatives of localities, are voted for only by sections of voters, or by local bodies of electors like the members of the state legislatures. There is no national party choice except that of President. No one else represents the people as a whole, exercising a national choice; and inasmuch as his strictly executive duties are in fact subordinated, so far at any rate as all detail is concerned, the President represents not so much the party's governing efficiency as its controlling ideals and principles. He is not so much part of its organization as its vital link of connection with the thinking nation. He can dominate his party by being spokesman for the real sentiment and purpose of the country, by giving direction to opinion, by giving the country at once the information and the statements of policy which will enable it to form its judgments alike of parties and of men.

For he is also the political leader of the nation, or has it in his choice to be. The nation as a whole has chosen him, and is conscious that it has no other political spokesman. His is the only national voice in affairs. Let him once win the admiration and confidence of the country, and no other single force can withstand him, no combination of forces will easily overpower him. His position takes the imagination of the country. He is the representative of no constituency, but of the whole people. When he speaks in his true character, he speaks for no special interest. If he rightly interpret the national thought and boldly insist upon it, he is irresistible; and the country never feels the zest of action so much as when its President is of such insight and calibre. Its instinct is for unified action, and it craves a single leader. It is for this reason that it will often prefer to choose a man rather than a party. A President whom it trusts can not only lead it, but form it to his own views.

It is the extraordinary isolation imposed upon the President by our system that makes the character and opportunity of his office so extraordinary. In him are centred both opinion and party. He may stand, if he will, a little outside party and insist as if it were upon the general opinion. It is with the instinctive feeling that it is upon occasion such a man that the country wants that nominating conventions will often nominate men who are not their acknowledged leaders, but only such men as the country would like to see lead both its parties. The President may also, if he will, stand within the party counsels and use the advantage of his power and personal force to control its actual programs. He may be both the leader of his party and the leader of the nation, or he may be one or the other. If he lead the nation, his party can hardly resist him. His office is anything he has the sagacity and force to make it.

Thus Mr. Wilson, before he was President, saw that the potentialities of the office were bounded only by the ability of the President for the time being to live up to the nation's expectations. It was in the same series of lectures, published as *Constitutional Government in the United States,* that Mr. Wilson repeated what he had said in 1900 in the Preface to the 15th edition of his *Congressional Government* (which I have already quoted): namely, that the Presidency itself had changed in character because of the Spanish War and the consequent entry of the American Republic into the arena of world affairs, in which the initiative of the President would inevitably enhance the prestige as well as the power of the office.

I have said elsewhere that the Presidency in its modern meaning, in its current concept, emerged under Theodore Roosevelt. The eighteenth century concept of the Chief Magistrate ended with John Quincy Adams. Andrew Jackson was both the leader and the symbol of the democratic revolt that made the President the choice of the mass of the voters at the polls and made the Presidency an instrument for the expression and enforcement of the national will. Of the Jackson school was Polk, of whom Mr. Wilfred E. Binkley has written: [2]

Perhaps the most remarkable testimony as to Polk's capacity as an executive fell half a century later from the lips of the last surviving

[2] *President and Congress,* by Wilfred E. Binkley. New York: Alfred A. Knopf, Inc., 1947, p. 100 ff.

member of his Cabinet, the eminent historian, George Bancroft. In 1887 Mr. Bancroft said that on the day of his inauguration Mr. Polk had told him that he had four definite objectives: the reduction of the tariff, the reestablishment of the independent treasury, the settlement of the Oregon boundary, and the acquisition of California. It is a matter of history that in all four of these he took the initiative before Congress assembled in its first session and carried out the first three of them in co-operation with Congress before the end of the session. The fourth was accomplished before the end of his term. Here is perhaps the finest example of the functioning of the Jacksonian type of Chief Executive. "His administration," wrote Bancroft, "viewed from the standpoint of results, was perhaps the greatest in our national history, certainly one of the greatest. He succeeded because he insisted on being its center and in overruling and guiding all his secretaries to act so as to produce unity and harmony."

After Polk, the prestige of the Presidency as well as the authority of the President declined as the nation came to grips with the slavery question that was to bring on the Civil War. A succession of relatively weak Presidents did not help to stave off catastrophe. The Civil War came, and the Union was saved by Mr. Lincoln because he used to the full not only all the Presidential powers to be found in the Constitution and the laws, but also some others that he appropriated to himself from elsewhere. In the retrospect the nation has honored him above all other Presidents for that sagacity and determination which saved the country by means which he himself had described in a letter written to A. G. Hodges on April 4, 1864: [3]

. . . I did understand, however, that my oath to preserve the Constitution to the best of my ability imposed upon me the duty of preserving, by every indispensable means, that government—that nation, of which that Constitution was the organic law. Was it possible to lose the nation and yet preserve the Constitution? By general law, life and limb must be protected, yet often a limb must be ampu-

[3] *Selections from Lincoln.* Nathaniel Wright Stephenson, editor. New York: Charles Scribner's Sons, Modern Student's Library, 1927, p. 400 ff.

tated to save a life; but a life is never wisely given to save a limb. I felt that measures otherwise unconstitutional might become lawful by becoming indispensable to the preservation of the Constitution through the preservation of the nation. Right or wrong, I assumed this ground, and now avow it. I could not feel that, to the best of my ability, I had even tried to preserve the Constitution, if, to save slavery or any minor matter, I should permit the wreck of government, country, and Constitution all together.

The Presidency once more went into eclipse after Lincoln; indeed, a hostile Congress, bent upon usurping the executive power to itself, all but destroyed the Presidency in its furious struggles with Andrew Johnson. The independence of the Executive Branch was reasserted and reestablished by two strong Presidents, Hayes and Cleveland, but, as I have said, the preponderance of political leadership was restored to it only after the war with Spain and when Theodore Roosevelt became its exponent.

Theodore Roosevelt was the first President I ever knew. My memory of my first meeting with him is vivid. I had been in Washington but a few weeks as the correspondent of two Southern newspapers, the *Nashville Banner* and the *Louisville Evening Post.* I was twenty-five years old, and regarded with awe the White House wherein had lived all the Presidents but Washington; and I stood in even greater awe of the man, the President of the United States, who to me was most of all the personified symbol of the Republic. I was too much a party Democrat not to have marked reservations with respect to Theodore Roosevelt the politician, but Theodore Roosevelt the President commanded my whole respect. I was not a little frightened and not a little nervous when I was shown into the Cabinet Room by Mr. William Loeb and asked to take a seat. Hardly had I done so when I sprang from it as the door opened and in burst not the President of the United States, but Teddy himself, flying coattails, flying eyeglass cord, gleaming teeth, squinting eyes, outstretched hand, and "DEE-lighted!"

He sat in his place at the head of the table and, waving at the customary seat of the Secretary of State, said "Take Mr. Hay's chair." In a moment I was at ease and under the spell of the charm. Then he asked me what in that day and time were the inevitable questions addressed to me by anybody acquainted with political history: "What relation are you to Parson Brownlow? What relation to Congressman Brownlow?" I hurriedly explained that not only was the cousinship distant, but that my father had not, like his distinguished editor-preacher cousin, stayed with the Union but had gone to the South and had served four years in the Rebel Army. This permitted him to claim kin with Georgia and the Confederate Navy through Admiral Bulloch. I think I even managed to squeak out that I personally was a Democrat, but he swept that aside because I was of much more importance to him, naturally, as the Washington correspondent of two papers, one of which, the *Louisville Evening Post,* was actively supporting his candidacy for the Republican nomination. Mr. Mark Hanna had died a week or ten days earlier, but his followers, "the Allies," as they were called, still hoped to prevent Roosevelt's nomination, still hoped to hit upon someone who would be more amenable to the orthodox Republican Party command which Mr. Hanna had captained. There was still some question how the Kentucky delegation would vote.

Theodore Roosevelt, the party candidate, appeared and jumped into the middle of things.

"I want you to let Dick Knott know that I am looking to him for leadership in winning Kentucky. If I had my way I would wipe out the present Republican leadership and reorganize the party under the command of such men as Dick Knott and Basil Duke."

I do not think he could possibly have said anything that would have been more distasteful to me. While I was a Democrat, I had the very highest respect for Mr. John W. Yerkes, who was then the leader of the regular Republican Party, and while I had a high professional esteem for the owner and editor of my own paper, Mr. Knott, the fact that he was a Gold Democrat rated him low indeed in my political scale. And as for Basil Duke, he was to me not only a renegade Gold Democrat but also the very personification of the railroad lobby in Frankfort, Kentucky.

Of course, I loyally transmitted Mr. Roosevelt's message to Mr. Knott, my editor, and my paper did valiant service in winning for Roosevelt the support of the Kentucky delegation—which I am persuaded Mr. Yerkes would have given to him anyway. Mr. Yerkes at that time was the Commissioner of Internal Revenue, and it was my habit to see him every morning; but of course I never told him what Teddy said.

I saw Mr. Roosevelt many other times in the White House, sometimes—as for instance during the struggle over the Hepburn Bill extending the powers of the Interstate Commerce Commission—quite frequently. He never again talked party politics to me, but from that first White House interview of mine with a President I have realized that party politics is and must be one of his prime concerns. He would not have got into the White House without it, he cannot stay there without it, and without it, when he comes to leave, he cannot expect any of the policies he has worked so hard to establish to be continued. But if the President maintains his political leadership, he has the opportunity, in some measure, to do the three things people expect of him as President: first, manage the machinery of government; second, engineer the economy of the nation; and third, represent the opinion of the people.

In speaking of the President as a manager of the machinery

of government, I am not limiting the function merely to the operation of the Executive Branch. Nor do I believe that the people impose any such limitation. In this connection, I remember talking once with Franklin D. Roosevelt about administration as distinguished from politics—and a particular phase of administration at that—the workload that devolved upon the President: the papers he had to read, the papers he had to sign, the letters he had to dictate, the things he had to do. Mr. Roosevelt said that perhaps it was not the office but the man that determined such things, although, of course, with the growth of the country and the increasing complexities of government it was in part the office. He told me that he had been talking just a few days before with Robert Lincoln O'Brien, one of Mr. Cleveland's secretaries, about the discussions that preceded and accompanied the introduction into the White House of a machine—by some people thought infernal—known as a typewriter. A similar palace revolution had taken place some years before (was it under Pierce, or Buchanan, or Lincoln?) when quill pens had been discarded for steel pens. It was under Woodrow Wilson (or was it Harding?) that the old wet press copybook was abandoned and carbon copies of letters were made instead. And under Wilson the correspondence began to be kept alphabetically, by name or by subject, in card indexes, instead of chronologically, in bound books. There were no fewer than 8,000 separate subject titles in F.D.R.'s letter files.

F.D.R. said there was no difficulty in Cleveland's time in taking care of all the correspondence with a few amanuenses, and that the President wrote most of his papers in longhand. Under Theodore Roosevelt, F.D.R. said there was a great deal more business; not all of it may have had anything particularly to do with government, as government was then understood, but there was a considerable amount of correspondence. Then, he said, although Wilson was a prolific letter-writer, and Hoover was a diligent devourer of documents, he was quite sure that he, F.D.R., every day had more letters to attend to than any of his predecessors; more pieces of business requiring his personal action every day than McKinley had had in a month.

Still on the topic of administrative work in the White House, F.D.R. said: "I learned a trick from Wilson. He once told me: 'If you want your memorandum read, put it on one page.' So I, when I came here, issued a similar decree, if you want to call it that. But even at that I am now forced to handle, so the oldsters around tell me, approximately a hundred times as many papers as any of my predecessors." Whether he was right, I do not know; but his certainly was a lively time what with crisis treading on the heels of crisis from deep depression to total war.

The expectancy is that the President will be the general manager of the entire machinery of government. It is true that if he undertakes this larger task with vigor and strength of will, he must needs assert himself in his capacity as Chief Legislator, he will have to recommend to the Congress measures that he deems expedient, he will have to report to the Congress on the state of the Union, and sometimes he will have to use or threaten to use his veto. At such times those of us who are opposed to his politics are apt to denounce him for attempting to reduce the Congress to the status of a rubber stamp, and will call him a dictator, and so on. But at the same time, if he does not get his policies adopted by the Congress, we say of him: "He has failed to get along with Congress."

Not only do we expect him to do more than administer the departments and win the assent of the Congress; we expect him also to manage in one way or another those great independent commissions which regulate certain aspects of our economic life, and which have been set up as quasi-legislative or quasi-judicial bodies with the express purpose of keeping them from being dominated by the President. If he attempts to meet this expectation of ours, and—even if successful—does it by the use of any public means or gesture, then with charming inconsistency we complain that he has overstepped the bounds of his office. Thus the President is compelled, in his efforts to meet this general expectation that he be the over-all general manager of the whole federal government, to consider the political expediency of each step he takes and to appraise the political implications of each act in terms not only of party, but also of popular and Congressional politics. As Pendleton Herring has said in his book, *Presidential Leadership*: [4]

We have created a position of great power but have made the full realization of that power dependent upon influence rather than legal authority. Hence if our president is to be effective, he must be a politician as well as a statesman. He must consider the political expedience of contemplated actions as well as their consistency with his concept of the public interest.

The element of contingency in our system is inherent in the uncertainty of party programs and party discipline. We are apparently willing to give popular support to a president while at the same time rejecting some of his most cherished measures. The president is titular head of the nation, chief legislator, and chief representative, as well as chief executive; we do not necessarily support him in all roles at the same time.

With respect to the narrower range of management, we expect him to coordinate the administrative policies of the far-flung, intricate, and complex maze of federal activities. But he knows that in his attempt to meet our expectations in this field he will encounter opposition, now from this pressure group and now from that; that he will encounter difficulties, now in this geographical section, now in that; that he will run into trouble,

---

[4] *Presidential Leadership,* by Pendleton Herring. New York: Farrar and Rinehart, Inc. (copyright now held by Rinehart & Co., Inc.), 1940, p. 2 ff.

now with his own party, now with the opposition. He knows that to the extent that he succeeds he will be denounced by some of us as an autocrat unwilling to delegate authority and to trust his own chosen subordinates. And equally well he knows that if he fails, practically all of us will say: "He was too weak for his job."

In this task of management of the machinery of government what we really expect and require of the President is, then, what has come to be known as top management. A top manager is one who exploits his position by whatever means he can devise to evoke the prime loyalty of divers parts of the great governmental machine, each part being also animated by a loyalty to its particular purpose. Thus the President must have, for example, at the head of the Departments of Agriculture, Commerce, and Labor men who are loyal to the principal purposes of the work entrusted to their departments, and who inevitably will express that departmental loyalty in conflicts of opinion among themselves, thus reflecting pressures from their particular supporters. But at the same time the President must resolve these particularistic differences and evoke the prime loyalty of these department heads to himself and the policies of his administration. Details of execution of these policies will be left to the lieutenants at lower echelons, but the President must be on top: he cannot delegate any part of that supreme task to another. He himself must be able to admonish and restrain his subordinates within his orbit and also be willing to protect and defend them from outside attack; and on occasion when particularistic loyalties overcome loyalty to the President, he must not hesitate to dismiss a lieutenant and choose another.

We have not put the President into this job as a top manager for the sake of giving him power over the largest and most complex machine in the world, or for the sake of giving someone we like and admire an opportunity to exhibit his skill of manipulation. But we have decided in the Constitution and the laws, in our customs and traditions, that one man and one alone may be top manager (just as we have decided that in war one man and one alone may be top commander) because that is the only way we think we can get results. We may not yet be willing to equip him properly for this job; we may not yet be willing to give him authority commensurate with his responsibilities for this task; but nevertheless we expect him to accomplish it.

Leaving aside for the moment the question of his authority and equipment, we see that here again what we expect of the President is leadership. Top management is not accomplished, even in small organizations, by requiring instant and implicit obedience to precise and particular commands. It is not accomplished by slavish adherence to rigid rules and precise procedures. Top management must, of course, employ the skills of scientific method, but in its expression it is the art of leadership. In a position of supreme responsibility such as that which rests on the President, this art will express itself in persuasiveness, in pervasive persuasiveness. In some Presidents this quality has been described as "charm" (in the case of Franklin D. Roosevelt), as a "winning way" (in the case of Woodrow Wilson), as "strenuosity" (in the case of Theodore Roosevelt). There was, too, the "whimsy" of Calvin Coolidge, but he did not choose to manage.

The second of the great things that we expect of our President is that he be a skilled engineer of the economy of the nation. Couched in the crudest form of political expression, the dictum runs that if the country is prosperous the President gets the credit, if it is not prosperous the President gets the blame. In its more subtle expression, our expectation of the President takes this form: We demand that he so manage the governmental machinery that we have good times and not hard times, and that the diverse sections of the economy be kept in reasonable balance; that in this part of his job the President act as the representative of all the people in the capacity of an impartial umpire rather than as Chief of State; and that he bring about this balanced prosperity through the exercise of his art of persuasion rather than through the exercise of his executive power.

When Mr. Madison in No. 10 of *The Federalist* discussed the problem raised by faction, and particularly economic faction, he found a republican remedy for it in the very extent and diversity of the federal system he was proposing and defending; but there is nothing to indicate that he foresaw the particular role of the President as the chief mediator among factions, and of course it was impossible for him to foresee the extent and complexity of the national economy in the mid-twentieth century. His classic description, however, may serve today: [5]

But the most common and durable source of factions has been the various and unequal distribution of property. Those who hold and those who are without property have ever formed distinct interests in society. Those who are creditors, and those who are debtors, fall under a like discrimination. A landed interest, a manufacturing interest, a mercantile interest, a moneyed interest, with many lesser interests, grow up of necessity in civilized nations, and divide them into different classes, actuated by different sentiments and views. The regulation of these various and interfering interests forms the principal task of modern legislation, and involves the spirit of party and faction in the necessary and ordinary operation of the government.

When I said that this description would serve as a statement of the problem which confronts a President in his role of chief engineer of our economy, I did not mean that I think it is complete. It will serve, perhaps, as a basic definition, but today we have to substitute our modern notions of what is property,

[5] *The Federalist,* No. 10, by James Madison. National Home Library Foundation Edition, 1938, p. 56.

and our twentieth century ideas of what are interests. Indeed, the Madison classic must be translated today into terms in which his interests divide by fission, each within itself, into conflicting interests. For instance, what was then a "manufacturing interest" is now management and labor, and this particular fission, observable in other activities besides manufacturing, is a principal problem of our economy today.

The President is expected to keep management and labor at peace and at the same time to keep industry in balance with agriculture and commerce. The struggle between the mercantile and the agrarian interests was not new when Washington took the oath as the first President; it was the small landowners who, banded together with the mechanics in the towns, overthrew the Federalists and brought Jefferson into the White House; it was the combination of small farmers and day laborers in the cities that ushered in Jackson and the Democratic revolution in 1828; the labor question, slave labor or free labor, divided the Republic almost from its beginning and all but destroyed it in the 1860's. The bankers, manufacturers, and merchants were hard pushed to elect McKinley over the crusading Bryan with his following of discontented farmers and laborers in 1896. Struggles of this kind are not new and they will not soon be ended.

Nevertheless, I think I am on safe ground in saying that not until the time of Theodore Roosevelt did the people of the country consciously expect the President to take the leadership in minimizing the detrimental effects on the public welfare of such conflicts. There had been occasional demands for Presidential action and occasional compliance with those demands, but they seem to have been exceptional.

It was in Theodore Roosevelt's administration that the people turned to the President to act not in his official capacity but as their representative to settle the great anthracite coal strike in Pennsylvania, to alleviate the effects of the banking crisis of

1907, and to prevent the threatened railroad strikes. To bring about a balance, a more equitable relationship among these varying groups, was the avowed purpose of the Square Deal of Theodore Roosevelt, of the New Freedom of Woodrow Wilson, of the New Deal of Franklin D. Roosevelt. It was also the avowed purpose of the other Presidents of this period, although they chose other methods. Only one of them, Herbert Hoover, gave his plan a name—the New Era.

After the first World War there was boom and there was bust. After the recovery from the bust there was inequality. The industrial regions prospered while the agricultural regions lagged. There was boom again and bust again, and then the great depression from '29 to '34, the recovery, the recession of '37, recovery again, and then World War II. Through all this, we have strengthened the emphasis we place on our expectations that the President engineer the national economy and maintain it in balance. And by gradual degrees we have formalized what we expect of the President in the realm of economic activity. In the administration of Herbert Hoover there was legislative sanction for the establishment of the Employment Stabilization Board. Later, the powers of this board were turned over to the National Resources Planning Board, which was set up in the Executive Office of the President during Franklin D. Roosevelt's administration. However, the Congress later abolished it because it was doing something that was deemed sinful: it had undertaken economic planning among other things. Now, under Truman, there has been set up in the Executive Office of the President the Council of Economic Advisers with which the President is expected to collaborate to present to the country and the Congress a continuing program for full employment, a continuing scheme for prosperity, a continuing guarantee against boom and bust. The powers now vested in the new Council of Economic Advisers, it should be mentioned, are practically the same as those of its predecessor, the National Resources Planning Board.

The third great thing that we expect of the President is that he be a faithful representative of the opinion of the people. The people are neither so naive nor so doctrinaire that they imagine the existence of one general opinion that reflects the views of the whole country. Rather they are insistent in their diverse groups that each group has the right opinion; that contrary opinions held by other groups are wrong; that the opinion of their group is right and should prevail as the national opinion; and that the way to bring about that desirable end is to persuade the President to go along with them. Here the processes of persuasion are reversed; they flow not outward from the White House but inward toward it. It is a centripetal, not a centrifugal, force.

Whether they meet as three people in a room or as 3,000 in a convention, the groups pass resolutions telling the President what to do; if they publish a journal, they publicly advise the President how to conduct himself; if they fear a rival group in a particular field, they hasten to claim from the President sole recognition as the representatives of their bailiwick.

One measure of the extent of this persuasive process of the people upon the President is provided by the size of the Presidential mailbag during various administrations. Just recently Mr. Ira Smith, who for fifty years, since McKinley, has been in charge of the mail room at the White House, was interviewed on the fiftieth anniversary of his service. He said that he, and he alone, took care of all mail that came to the President from McKinley's time until the end of the Hoover administration. During that time there had been two peaks. One was in the administration of Theodore Roosevelt, when during the anthracite coal strike the letters for a short time got up to a thousand a day. People did not write very much to Mr. Taft, and during his administration the volume dropped to about 200 a week. Then Wilson came in and the letters went up to an average of a thousand a day during periods of crisis, dropping off after he became ill. They dropped again under Mr. Hoover, and Mr. Smith, having no aid at all, took care of all the letters.

Then F.D.R. came in. One sentence at the conclusion of his inaugural address—"We have nothing to fear but fear itself"— so electrified the nation, recreating its hopes, that it alone brought into the White House 460,000 letters. The Presidential mailbag grew to such proportions that Mr. Smith had to get two additional rooms in the State Department building and accumulate a staff of 50 persons to help him. Throughout the entire twelve years of Franklin D. Roosevelt's administration, the average was more than 5,000 letters a day. It rose at times on the March of Dimes birthday celebration to as high as 150,000 to 175,000 a day. In times of great crises, it would frequently run as much as 25,000 a day for a week. The average of 5,000 over the twelve years of Franklin Roosevelt's administration includes a great falling off in the war years, when sometimes there would be a week or two with only 2,000 or 3,000 letters a day.

The mail under the Truman administration is continuing at about the rate that it was toward the end of the Roosevelt administration, something around 4,000 letters a day. In this huge body of correspondence that flows to the White House all kinds of views and desires find expression. Not all of the letters are written in praise. Many of them are full of denunciation or admonition; some again are appeals for assistance or special consideration.

It must not be imagined, however, that in this category of expectations that the people expect the President to represent them only in political matters or economic matters. They press upon him all sorts of things. They extract from him proclamations for Mother's Day, and for Be Kind to Animals Week. They expect him to express their opinion with respect to the necessity of contributing to the Community Chest and see to it that a properly formulated letter is submitted to the White House for his signature. He is sore beset by these importunities. He knows that he must in a measure meet this expectation, but he knows also that at any moment in one of these seemingly minor matters he may stub his toe. Yet the President must always be aware of this third great expectation—that he reflect public opinion. It is addressed not to the party chieftain, not to the head of the government, but to the Chief of State, the man who is the symbol of the nation.

These three expectations I have been examining are great indeed, but they represent simply the methodological aspects of accredited and acknowledged leadership. If the President fails as a leader or if, as he sometimes does, he rejects the role of leader and insists upon keeping himself confined to his strictly legal, strictly constitutional, strictly official duties, then the pressure of the public will be withdrawn, but at the cost of a sense of loss. In that sense of loss the people turn to the future and to the successor of the President, as they did turn from Taft and from Hoover, neither of whom so much failed to lead as refused to lead.

In the endowment of leadership by Constitution and custom, there remains, however, the greatest expectation of all. It is the expectation that the President, with his unquestioned responsibility for maintaining the initiative in foreign affairs, shall keep us at peace; but that if war does come, he shall as Commander-in-Chief lead us to victory. Here again we fail to give him authority commensurate with his responsibility, but despite this failure to provide him with the means of accomplishing what we ask him to do, we still expect the President to give effect to the national purpose.

Reluctantly, tardily, we have apparently come to the conclusion that peace is not a thing apart, but that it must be achieved in a concert of nations. The United States is now a member of the United Nations. And as a consequence of that new relationship the people of the United States now expect their President to do even more. Whether out of pride or out of trepidation, we believe our country to be the greatest nation in the world; we expect our President to lead the nation; we expect him to assume the leadership of the world.

[IV]

How We Control the President

IF, AS I HAVE SAID, we as a people consider the Presidency to be an inexhaustible fountain from which we may demand everything and anything that we desire; if we do as a people require the President to manage our governmental business, to engineer our national economy, and to reflect our opinions faithfully; if we do as a people expect him to be a leader, the leader of his party, the nation, and even the world; if we as a people expect all these things, it by no means follows that we are in the slightest degree willing to permit him to do them in his own time and in his own way.

He may be our leader but he is at the same time our servant; we may ask him to lead us, but we see to it that we control him.

His powers, though great, are defined in a written Constitution; his authority, though wide, is established by law; and his discretion, though extended downward to matters of minute detail and upward into the widest ranges of policy, is subject to review. If he steps outside the bounds of legality, his acts are subject to invalidation, and if he impinges on private rights, a review of his action may be initiated by the humblest citizen of the Republic. And, of course, the Congress is always there to check him; the courts are always there to curb him.

Then, too, while the President is the Chief of State and, under Constitutional control, is clothed with the power and authority necessary to perform the numerous duties implied by that designation, the very State of which he is the head is not itself absolute. It is a federal republic and many of the things that we popularly expect the President to do are not within the scope of his authority, are not indeed within the scope of the authority of the Executive Branch of the federal government, but have been reserved to the states or to the people. More than that, our system is not only federal but dual; it is predicated on the theory of popular sovereignty. "We, the people" (in various forms of expression, of course), established not only the Constitution of the United States but the constitution of each of the forty-eight states; and this duality is complete and without hierarchical relationships.

The President, as the head of the Executive Branch, has no representatives in the states, each of which has its own executive branch headed by a popularly elected Governor to whom the people of his own state have entrusted varying grants of power. The effective privilege of citizenship in the one system does not necessarily depend upon the other; the right to vote, for instance, is a right not enjoyed by any citizen of the United States as such. In order to vote he must also become a citizen of a state. While no state now is permitted to discriminate in granting the franchise on account of race, color, or sex, states still are free to make other discriminations, such as those based on age or property. States may even, if they desire, grant the franchise to those who are not citizens of the United States, a practice that was common half a century ago when many of the states gave the right to vote to immigrants who had taken out their "first papers" and who often would have to wait as long as four years to become citizens of the United States. It was not until the adoption of the Fourteenth Amendment in 1868 that citizenship in the United States necessarily carried with it citizenship in the state of residence.

It is true that this duality of structure in such complete form was not envisaged by the Founding Fathers. Indeed, the states as states were given control of the upper house of the Congress, and the legislatures of the states elected the Senators. In the earlier days of the Republic state legislatures frequently undertook to instruct their U. S. Senators how to vote on pending measures, and some Senators whose consciences would not support their carrying out these instructions would resign.

The Seventeenth Amendment providing for the election of Senators by the people came into effect in May, 1913. However, the citizens of the states as states retained a measure of control by reason of the fact that each state has equal representation in the Senate regardless of its size, and no state can be deprived of that equality without its consent.

The President is controlled not only by the Congress acting as the legislature enacting the laws which the President is bound to execute, and appropriating the funds with which he executes them: the Senate also exercises a high degree of control over the President through its sharing with him of a large part of the executive power.

All of the Constitutional and legal controls to which the President is subjected fall into two categories. His general powers and his ordinary grants of authority are to be found in the Constitution itself and in the statutes enacted by the Congress, which he is bound to carry into execution; but his specific authority to administer these general powers and perform these general duties is furthermore and specifically limited by the control of funds by the Congress and by the subjection of the Presidential power of appointment to office and negotiation of treaties to the Senate. His appointments of principal officers (and it is the Congress which decides which officers are principal) are subject to confirmation by a majority vote of the Senate; and the treaties he negotiates with foreign powers require the consent of two-thirds of the Senate to their ratification.

Thus it is that there are always two general fields in which the Congress and the President are engaged either in conflict or in a process of adjustment. One is that of general legislation in which, for the most part, the differences of opinion take on the aspect of party politics or else reflect sectional or interest group divisions. The other is that of its specific annual grant of funds in which party politics is subordinated to the program politics of varying economic opinions of the departmental, bureaucratic, and pressure group concerns.

There is a different field of conflict or of search for adjustment between the President and the Senate. Here the conflict may become fierce and of great importance. In the case of treaties, where one-third plus one of the Senators voting may negate the executive action, mighty battles have been waged, in many of which the President has been defeated. Here he must command more than mere party support. Indeed, I think there has been only one instance since the parties were established in which any one party had more than two-thirds of the Senators, and during that brief period of two years from 1937 to 1939, no important treaties were submitted to the Senate. General Washington walked out of the Senate chamber when he encountered difficulties regarding ratification of a treaty with an Indian tribe and swore that he would never go back there again. Polk, failing to get his treaty with the Republic of Texas ratified, bypassed the two-thirds rule by getting an executive agreement confirmed by both Houses of Congress. The treaty of peace with Spain was ratified by a margin of only one vote after William Jennings Bryan had exerted to the full his persuasive powers as the leader of the minority party, in support of President McKinley's treaty. And no one needs to be reminded of the defeat of Woodrow Wilson and his League of Nations at the hands of a minority of hostile Senators.

In the matter of confirmation of appointments, the control exercised by the Senate over the President is perhaps even as important, since it is stringent and continuous and but rarely boils up to the point where the public is aware of it. While the Senate usually confirms his appointments as members of the Cabinet, ambassadors, and members of the Supreme Court—even when the President's political party is in the minority—this is not the case with respect to judges of circuit and district courts, district attorneys, United States marshals, and the like. These high officers who are subject to confirmation, for the most part also fall within the rule of senatorial courtesy; the Senators, being of the majority party in the state in which the judge or district attorney will function, have by courtesy the right of proscription, and except in extraordinary cases the Senate will refuse confirmation to anyone they object to, and indeed anyone whom any Senator objects to as being "personally obnoxious." This means that in practice the President does not choose these district judges and district attorneys, collectors of internal revenue, and the like. The Senators choose them and the President's power is reduced to the status of a veto. He can, of course, refuse to send up the name of a man of whom he disapproves, but he knows it is useless to send up one of whom the Senators disapprove.

Of late years the Senate has endeavored more than once to extend its control over these appointments and virtually to take the appointing power away from the President, by fixing a certain limit of salary or compensation as the determining factor requiring senatorial confirmation. Thus the requirement that anybody who received compensation in excess of $4,000 in the Federal Emergency Relief Administration would have to be confirmed by the Senate actually operated to take the appointing power of relief officials away from the President and vest it in particular Senators from particular states. The House of Representatives is often reluctant to join in this extension of senatorial patronage, and it is to the House that the President must look for his principal defense against this particular type of usurpation, since he is all but deprived of the defense of his own veto by the circumstance that such patronage forays are always imbedded in the heart of the appropriation bills.

Sometimes the controls set up to check and curb the President seem to end in an open quarrel between the President and the Congress, in which each seems to be contending for absolute domination over the other. It would, in my opinion, clarify public discussion of the way our institutions operate if we were more particular in defining the contending parties in these public disputes. Sometimes indeed it is the President against the Congress, sometimes it is the President against the Senate only, and sometimes it is, oddly enough, simply a situation in which the President is drawn into a quarrel between the Senate and the House.

What we have done deliberately as a people in the Constitution and in the laws, by means of the Congressional power of the purse and by means of the senatorial review of appointments and of treaties, is to give effect to the theory of checks and balances. We have vested the executive power in the President, we control his exercise of that power by the Congress, and we curb both the President and the Congress from wanton invasion of the rights of the people by means of the Court. However, the machinery with which we control the President is by no means confined to this formalized system of checks and balances. We undertake also to control him by custom and tradition and by subjecting him in many ways to the direct impact of the voice of the people as interpreted by this, that, or the other special interest.

The President's own Cabinet officers and all of their subordinates in their day-to-day work of administration come in contact with the people, and especially with the particular groups which they directly serve, and through them the wishes of the people are transmitted in a continuous flow upward to the President. He cannot escape this flood of advice. And only he can coordinate it into a single national policy—however flexible that may prove to be.

The engines through which these extralegal controls exert their compulsion upon the President are exceedingly numerous and defy classification. Most of them exert their power or attempt to do so not only upon the President but upon his party and upon the members of that party in the Congress. When these interests, big and little, and of almost infinite diversity, seek to influence the government, they quite naturally identify their own special interest with the general public welfare of the entire country. This rationalization permits them to demand of the President and the members of his party in the Congress compliance with their desires on pain of withdrawal of political support, on pain of punishment at the polls in the next election. The same rationalization permits the same groups to demand of the President his support for compliance on the ground that he is the leader of the nation and hence above party. In this way the President is subjected to an enfilading fire. His party colleagues in the Congress may take refuge behind a localized or sectional sentiment in a particular Congressional district or state, but the President occupies a position so exposed that no such defense is available to him.

The means by which these extralegal and popular ways of control reach the President fall perhaps into three general categories: 1) the press, including the radio; 2) the post office and the telegraph; and 3) the public opinion polls. Of these three the press is easily the most powerful and most important and has been a principal factor in our national policy from the earliest days, long antedating the Constitution and the establishment of the Presidency. The post office, too, is older than the Presidency, and the process of influencing politics through the writing of letters has been a conspicuous part of our American life at least from the times when the Committees of Correspondence stirred up the colonies to take the unified action that brought about the Revolution and independence. The public opinion polls are relatively new. In the form of straw votes to indicate the probable result of coming elections they had their beginning shortly after the Civil War, but it was not until the Franklin D. Roosevelt administration was well under way that serious efforts were made through a sampling process to measure the trends of public opinion in the country on all sorts of questions, social and economic as well as political. However, while the letter writers and the newspaper publishers have been with us from the beginning, their methodology has changed, and many of the manifestations of their power or lack of it are of recent origin.

Furthermore, these engines are influenced by each other. For instance, a paid advertisement of a pressure group in a daily newspaper may send a flood of letters and telegrams to the White House advocating a course of action strongly opposed by that very newspaper; the publication of a public opinion poll will produce letters of protest against the trend recorded by the poll. And in their turn, the newspapers and the radio broadcasters take the letter writers and the poll takers into consideration in their programs.

As we have seen, by far the mightiest of these engines is the press which now, of course, includes the radio. In the early days of the Republic and, indeed, until the time of Theodore Roosevelt, in whose administration, as I have said, the modern manifestation of the Presidency made its appearance, the Presidents were concerned with editorial opinion much more than with news, and from the earliest days every President excepting perhaps only Washington made use of the press maintained by his own political party to defend himself from the attacks of the opposition party press. Presidents and aspirants to the Presidency kept their own newspapers and their own editors, maintaining them by subsidies of one sort or another, public place or public printing, delivered to them by the Presidents, or promised to them by Presidential aspirants. This led to an intensely partisan press which developed a pattern that spread from the large cities to the small towns, even to country villages, for there were political jobs and public printing contracts in states, counties, and cities as well as in Washington.

After the Civil War, or perhaps more precisely after the reconciliation achieved under President Hayes, the press began to be more independent; more and more newspapers began to pride themselves on being independent and nonpartisan; more and more editors began to wear with pride the title of Mugwump, which their fellows had flung at them in derision. In the great and significant Presidential election of 1896 the press overwhelmingly supported McKinley and denounced Bryan, and thereafter the clear distinction between a Republican and a Democratic paper became more and more difficult to make.

While I have been discussing the press as a principal means whereby the people control the President through the power of public opinion, it must not be imagined that this avenue accommodates only one-way traffic. For by the same token, the press is the principal engine which the President uses to influence public opinion, to maintain discipline in his own party, and to spread dissension among the opposition. Theodore Roosevelt was not, of course, the first President either to use the press for his own purposes or to be affected by it. All his predecessors save only Washington had had similar experiences. But Theodore Roosevelt was the first President to grasp the significance of the great change that was taking place in the

American press. Before his time, practically all politicians had placed the greatest emphasis upon editorial opinion, supported now and again by political correspondents and the publication of political speeches. Roosevelt saw that more and more the people were being affected by the news, that more and more the people were making up their own minds on the basis of what they considered to be their own knowledge of what was going on.

For the first time the White House became a prime news source. It was Teddy who saw Big Bill Price hanging about the White House gates in all sorts of weather, waiting to get news from the White House visitor on his way out, and it was Teddy who took Big Bill Price out of the rain and the sun and installed him in a tiny press room in the small new office addition attached to the West Wing of the White House. The press galleries had been appurtenances of the two Houses of the Congress almost from the beginning, but this was the first recognition by a President that news gathering was a legitimate occupation and news giving a legitimate obligation of the highest office of the State. Nowadays Theodore Roosevelt is sometimes credited with holding press conferences, but the phrase "press conference" was not invented until after his time; nor did the connotation of that phrase as used today—that it is open to all the press—apply in Roosevelt's case.

Theodore Roosevelt was picky and choosey with respect to his newspapermen. If a particular paper offended him—and many of them did—he refused to see any representative of that paper. If a particular correspondent offended him—and many of them did—he forbade him the run of the White House and ordered the executive departments to give him no news. Not only that, but Teddy would publicly thrust him into the Ananias Club. Theodore Roosevelt had something of a systematic press scheme organized around the correspondents of the news services, but in addition to this he had a group of personal friends and favorites among the newspaper men who saw him frequently and through whom he used to send up his trial balloons to test public opinion. To those of us who were neither of the inner circle nor the outcast, these were "cuckoos" or the "fairhaired boys." I am told that within the precincts of the Ananias Club they were considered something else again.

Looking back over forty years and more since I first walked into the White House in quest of news, I believe that the most astonishing measure of the immense and at that time unimaginable growth of our government is the fact that the government of Theodore Roosevelt's time just did not make enough news to satisfy either the President or his newspaper friends. The activities of the whole government were not enough to turn up even one tolerably good news item a week, let alone enough for two whole press conferences a week.

Theodore Roosevelt early learned many things about newspapers, one of them being that there is a bear market in big headlines on Monday mornings, and that therefore Monday morning is the time to garner sheaves of publicity. He liked the publicity and, not being willing to wait until there was enough governmental news to pay for it, he entered other fields in order to maintain his manifest right to the big Monday morning headline. Thus we had from him disquisitions on simplified spelling, race suicide, the strenuous life, and the like. Of if there was no news within the government he would manufacture it by a Presidential denunciation, couched in furious and violent language, of some "malignant malingerer," some "malefactor of great wealth," some "detestable liar." But for all of that, the President conceived of his relations with a newspaper correspondent as personal, and the correspondents on their part conceived of their access to the White House as a privilege and not a right.

Mr. Taft was not so successful with the press. It is still difficult for me to understand how one who had been so genial and approachable when he was Secretary of War, who had been accustomed to meeting newspapermen every day, and who gave out news without any apparent reluctance or restraint, could have been changed so much by becoming President. The same observation may be made of Mr. Hoover, who certainly had a good press when he was Secretary of Commerce but was not able to keep it long in the White House. Perhaps no other two Presidents of this era have been so maladroit in their relations with the press. And, in my opinion, no other Presidents of this modern era have so completely ignored the press in making up their minds with respect to public policy.

It remained for Woodrow Wilson to institutionalize the relations between the White House and the newspapers. Within a few days after his inauguration, he established the regular press conference, open to newspapermen as a matter of right and not as a matter of personal privilege. He accepted the press as a two-way avenue of communication, from the President to the people and from the people to the President. No correspondent was excluded from these conferences because of the political complexion of his newspaper or of his publisher, although more than one publisher vainly sought the privilege of a private interview with Mr. Wilson. It was Woodrow Wilson also who first institutionalized the receiving end of the White House press relations. Theodore Roosevelt had been an omnivorous reader of the newspapers and his secretariat gave him clippings to read. Mr. Taft frequently refused to read any newspaper that disagreed with him and was impatient of those about him who urged him to find out what the other side was doing or saying. Mr. Wilson, however, had his secretariat begin the work of clipping news, editorial comments, and cartoons from papers all over the country; then these clippings were pasted on sheets of yellow paper, and the resulting "Yellow Journal," as it soon was nicknamed, was laid on the President's desk. That, of course, was but a small forerunner of the elaborate index of news and opinion that under F.D.R. became a part of the regular White House office routine. Every President since Woodrow Wilson has, in different forms and varying lengths of time, continued the institution of the formal press conference. Mr. Wilson stopped it, however, when the United States went into World War I in 1917, and its adoption by President Harding, a former newspaper publisher, was therefore looked upon as a revival rather than as a continuation of a White House procedure.

Mr. Wilson had permitted oral questions from any correspondent without previous notice and had replied extemporaneously to them, subject only to the rule that he was not to be directly quoted without specific permission. Mr. Harding at first followed this example, but when during the Naval Disarmament Conference in Washington he got mixed up as to whether Japan was to be considered merely as a group of islands or as essentially a part of the Asiatic mainland, and the Secretary of State, Mr. Charles E. Hughes, was forced to correct him, he changed the rules and thereafter required questions to be written out and submitted in advance.

Mr. Coolidge, who managed to keep cool with the press, required written questions submitted in advance, replied only to such of them as he chose, and invented the "White House spokesman" as a ghostly vehicle for his own expressions. Mr. Hoover also required written questions submitted in advance, but toward the end of his term he held fewer and fewer press conferences, and finally dropped them altogether.

Under F.D.R., the press conference was revived and revitalized. Any person certified as a legitimate correspondent by the correspondents themselves, acting through their own association, was admitted to the conferences. Anyone might ask any question, although the President reserved the right to answer in his own way, and again there was but the one rule that no direct quotation be made without express permission. The White House instantly became the No. 1 news source of the nation, and so it has remained to this day. Franklin D. Roosevelt had had the experience of the early Wilson press conferences. He had repeated the experiment for himself in the Governor's office in Albany, and he did not shrink from the ordeal as had his immediate predecessors in the White House. Indeed, for him the press conference was no ordeal but an opportunity to influence opinion that he accepted with alacrity and evident zest.

By his time the government of the United States had become so big and complex and the problems it dealt with had become so tremendous in importance and bulk that there was never any need for F.D.R. to take excursions into outside matters in order to make the Monday morning headlines. During his time in the White House more things happened that were "newsworthy" than had happened in the administrations of all his predecessors together, and in the course of the little more than twelve years that Franklin D. Roosevelt was President he made public statements or comments through the agency of the White House press conference upon a greater number of public questions than had all his predecessors together.

As did every one of his predecessors in this modern era beginning with Theodore Roosevelt, F.D.R. had his quarrels with the press. He was not quite so violent perhaps in his expressions as was his distant cousin whom he so fondly called Uncle Ted. He was not so choleric as Taft, not so icily disdainful as Wilson, not so pathetically imploring as Harding, not so calculating as Coolidge, nor so embittered as Hoover, when each in his own time and way complained about unfair treatment at the hands of the newspapers. He was, however, apt to be more selective and discriminating as among particular newspapers on the one hand, and as between publishers and working newspapermen on the other. For the greater part of his three terms and a few months in office, he also had a greater numerical proportion of the newspaper press of the country opposed to him than did any of his predecessors. Despite that, because of his superb sense of news and of timing, he managed to keep his own point of view in the news columns of most of the newspapers, whatever their editorial opinion may have been.

Then, too, F.D.R. was the first President to realize the value of the radio as a direct channel of communication from the President to the people. It had been used by Presidential candidates in campaigns—by Hoover and Smith in 1928, and by Hoover and Roosevelt in 1932. But the institution of the Fireside Chat brought the President into the homes of the people as nothing had ever done before. At the same time as the press and the radio, its younger sister, were compelled by Presidential initiative to look more and more to the White House as a prime source of news, so they in turn compelled the President to look more and more to them as the agents through which effective public opinion might be brought to bear upon him. Then the newspapers, acting cooperatively, began to publish the results of public opinion polls. That these polls have had a great effect upon the consideration of public questions in the White House cannot be doubted. These polls measure the popularity of the President in office and they measure the relative popularity of the two great political parties, as well as test opinion with respect to current questions. Many and long are the discussions with respect to their accuracy, but thus far their straw votes taken in advance of elections have established a sufficiently high record of accuracy to give all of their results great weight amongst those whose chief business it is to study the trends of public opinion in the country.

When Mr. Roosevelt died and Mr. Truman succeeded him there was great curiosity about what would happen to the press conference. What did happen, of course, was that the institution was continued as it had been in the early Wilson days and under Franklin D. Roosevelt, with the exception that its frequency was reduced. Oddly enough, in the first of the Truman conferences the assembled reporters seemed to assume a sort of protective air. They complained that "Harry was too quick with his answers," that he shot too often from the hip, that he did not seem to know how to take sufficiently evasive action. Thus the correspondents of newspapers and radio have become so jealous of the White House press and radio conference as an institution that they seem to be at pains to protect it even from what they feared might be the ineptitude of its chief performer, the President himself. Of late, such complaints have not been heard.

It would be almost impossible, in my opinion, for any President now to change this pattern or to interfere in any material way with this informal White House institution, set up without authority of law, required by no Constitutional mandate, embodying no rights enforceable in a court of law, but nevertheless an institution of prime importance in the political life of the American people.

The White House has become not only the prime source of news for the United States but one of the principal news sources for all the nations of the world. Some of those Americans who have seemed to doubt from time to time the excellence of the Presidential system as compared with the parliamentary system in a democratic nation have made much of the efficacy of the device of control which they imagine to be exerted by individual members of the parliament over the executive by means of the question hour in parliament. They have said that if our Cabinet officers and our heads of departments were to come on the floor of the House or the Senate and there answer questions, the people would know more about their government than they do. In my opinion, these critics of the Presidential system are mistaken. No question-time interrogation in the British Parliament, for instance, can compare with the intensive interrogation given to heads of departments and their subordinates by a Congressional committee. But if it be objected that these questions and answers are sometimes in camera, there can be no doubt that the questions put by newspaper correspondents and the answers made by the President in the White House press conference are public property, as public as any newspaper correspondent or radio commentator may wish.

President Roosevelt considered at one time the exclusion of matters respecting foreign affairs from the scope of the press conference, but he wisely, in my opinion, rejected the suggestion and kept it open and free. That this entails dangers no one can doubt. That this open forum is used from time to time by the enemies of the President to embarrass him or his administration is unquestionably true.

On the other hand, it is also true, in my opinion, that in the institution of the White House press and radio conference the President reaches the people and the people reach the President more easily and more quickly than in any other way that has yet been devised. Thus the White House press conference is one of the most important of all American institutions because it gives the people as a whole a measure of direct control over the one elected official who represents all the people and because it gives the President, the one elected representative of all the people, direct communication with the individual members of his constituency.

[v]

How We Equip the President for His Task

WE, THE PEOPLE OF THE United States, vest the executive power of the government in the President. As we have seen, we expect him to do many things for us. We are disappointed and grieved when he fails to do the things that we expect of him at the time and in the manner we desire. We expect him to right the things that are wrong and to champion the cause to which we are devoted. If he fails us we will condemn him without mercy, though we know that in most matters he cannot please everyone and must engender opposition and make enemies. We continue to exercise over him, as we have seen, many types of control, intimate, detailed, and rigorous; some of them inherent in our Constitution, some of them established by law, and many more set up by tradition and custom and enforced by public opinion.

For the most part we think of him only as a national political leader, and we judge him to be right or wrong in the terms of the policies he pursues and the course of action that he espouses. We but seldom think of him as the chief administrator, as the manager-in-chief, as the occupant of the Presidency, which is our only Constitutional means of coordinating the vast and complex structure of the Executive Branch of the government.

Here, perhaps, lies the root cause of the fact that the equipment we give the President to do his work is so meager. We do not endow him with authority commensurate with his responsibility. We do not equip him with the means to meet our expectations, and since this lack is so seldom recognized by those of us who are bent upon this, that, or the other political, economic, or social policy, the problem falls outside the realm of the emotions. The problem here being discussed is not "*what* the President should do*,*" but "*how* he can do it." We cannot expect to bring to its consideration the fervor and devotion that can be commanded when the problem is one of *what* to do. The problem of "how to do" falls more within the intellectual than the emotional realm. It is harder to think than it is to feel, and it is very much harder to think about things that seem to be but unimportant details than it is to feel about the things that seem most important to us. So manifest is this predisposition of ours to elevate the political consideration, the *what* to do, above the administrative consideration of *how* to do it, that even on the rare occasions when administrative questions do rise to a level where they are subject to general and popular discussion, very frequently that discussion will go off at a tangent whose direction is determined by some political, even some partisan or pressure group, interest.

All this has been true from the beginning. This is not the place nor am I the person to review the varying interpretations that have been given to the Constitutional establishment of the executive, nor to retell the long story of the struggles between the President and the Congress for preponderant control. But taking a narrower and more restricted view and considering the problem primarily in relation to the Presidency, it may be useful to sketch the administrative history of the federal government.

The Constitution said of the President: ... "he may require the Opinion, in writing, of the principal Officer in each of the executive Departments, upon any Subject relating to the Duties of their respective Offices ..." Implicit in this passage is an assumption by the Constitutional Convention which created the Executive, the Legislative, and the Judicial Branches that the executive departments then in being under the Articles of the Constitution would as a matter of course be continued. These departments then were the Department of Foreign Affairs, Treasury, War, and Post Office. The new Constitution did not abolish those departments; it simply created an executive power which did not theretofore exist and vested it in a President. The executive departments continued to function as the Convention, the first Congress, and the first President evidently expected them to do until their successors might be organized under the new Constitutional system—something that was not accomplished until many months after George Washington had taken the oath as the first President of the United States.

Before the departments were organized under the new Constitutional arrangement, Washington required the opinions in writing of these principal officers. He continued to do so after the departments had been organized by statute and furnished with funds duly appropriated by the Congress. He added, however, an arrangement of his own: he invited three of them, the heads of the Departments of State (formerly called Foreign Affairs), Treasury, and War to meet in consultation with him. This was the genesis of the President's Cabinet, although it was not so called for a long time. Indeed, it has not at any time ever had either Constitutional or legal sanction, and exists only at the pleasure of the President for the time being.

In the early days, the principal officers or heads of departments were ordinarily referred to in Congressional debate and popular conversation as ministers. Collectively, therefore, it was easy to think of them as constituting a ministry, and it was equally easy for the House of Representatives, which then thought of itself as the principal legislative body, to expect the ministers to report to it. Similarly, it was easy at that time for the Senate, consisting of at most 26 persons, to think of itself more as an executive council, advisory to the President, than as the upper house of the legislature.

The President was above party, and indeed there was but one party in the Congress. Those who had opposed the Federalists in their capacity as revolutionaries had been suppressed or even exiled. Those who had opposed the Federalists in their capacity as proponents of the new Constitution simply had been left at home. But there was discernible the beginning of faction, the germ of partisan division, and the President held himself austerely above faction, above the nascent parties, and sought to achieve the aims of the Executive Branch by inviting into his council the two revolutionary leaders of opposing views: the liberal Jefferson to be Secretary of State, the conservative Hamilton to be Secretary of the Treasury. Soon these two men not only were in a struggle to determine the direction of policy, but they were also in a squabble concerning the jurisdiction of their two departments.

Eventually these struggles and squabbles extended into the halls of both Houses of Congress. The primary result was the creation of two parties, Federalist and Anti-Federalist. A secondary result was the assumption by the Congress of the power to determine the jurisdictional scope of each of the executive departments, a determination that perhaps was inevitable in view of the ambiguity of the Constitution and in view of the very nature of the power of the purse, unquestionably in the control of the Legislative Branch of the government.

By the time Washington retired—certainly by the time John Adams gave way to Jefferson—the essential features of the administrative organization of the government were established in the form in which, in the main, they exist today; a form which perpetuates ambiguity that long ago should have been clarified; a form which admits, if it does not invite, many futile, useless, and wasteful jurisdictional squabbles between the Executive and the Legislative Branches and among the departments and divisions of the Executive Branch. Efforts to improve this pattern have been made from time to time. Some of them have met with some small measure of success, but in view of what the people require of the President and expect him to do, no small part of the inevitable and inescapable tragedy that envelops that high position arises from the fact that the structural machinery of the Executive Branch is still that devised in the closing days of the eighteenth century.

If we take this structure in its classic form, ignoring for the moment the changes resulting from the Civil Service Act of 1883, the Budget and Accounting Act of 1921, and the Reorganization Act of 1939, and postponing also for the moment consideration of the independent regulatory agencies, we discover that the President is equipped with a number of executive departments upon which he relies for help not only in the day-to-day operation of the government but in the exercise of his Constitutional duty to take care that the laws are faithfully executed.

The principal feature of the machinery with which we equip the Presidency to perform its tasks is the Cabinet. Extra-Constitutional, extralegal, essentially amorphous, and utterly lacking in continuity, the Cabinet changes with every incoming President, not only in personnel but in character as well. Nevertheless, subject as it is to the changes that are inherent in the personality and working habits of each new President, the Cabinet has come to have a certain traditional investiture of form. It is made up of heads of departments who operate the vast administrative machinery of the government and who, being brought together with the President at the Cabinet table in the Cabinet Room of the White House, constitute the President's Cabinet, which then becomes a council of advisers considered to be "official" in character, notwithstanding its lack of any legal authority. This traditional pattern, which was established by George Washington, has been continued until this day and is even more resistant to change, perhaps, than if it had been set up as an institution by law.

From time to time during the years, as government has moved into new areas, it has been the practice for Congress to set up a new bureau or division, usually within one of the departments, but sometimes as an independent agency, and then later, as the new function has become a part of the accepted order of things, to establish a new department to contain that function. The Postmaster General and the Attorney General were brought early into the Cabinet by invitation of the President: the Post Office Department had existed before the Constitution, but the Department of Justice was not organized until some time after the Attorney General had sat in the Cabinet. The Navy was taken out of the jurisdiction of the War Department and set up as a separate Navy Department. A Home Department was established into which could be gathered a number of bureaus not appropriate for existing departments or which were operating without supervision, and the name soon was changed to Department of the Interior. The heads of these seven departments formed the Cabinet in Lincoln's time. The immediate supervision of the operating functions of their departments was their primary administrative responsibility, but collectively they formed a council of advisers to the President.

But as an executive council they had advisory functions only, as is witnessed by the famous story of Lincoln's putting a question to a vote in the Cabinet. On that occasion each of the seven Cabinet members voted no. Lincoln voted aye and then announced the result: "Ayes one, noes seven. The ayes have it." There is indeed some evidence to substantiate the tradition that John Quincy Adams sometimes put matters of policy to a vote in the Cabinet and considered himself bound by the result, but no other President has considered himself thus bound.

Under Cleveland there was created the Department of Agriculture, under Theodore Roosevelt the Department of Commerce and Labor, and under Taft that Department was divided into two Departments, of Commerce and Labor respectively, a separation which became effective with the inauguration of Wilson. These ten departments, each constituted by an Act of Congress, today compose what is called the "official Cabinet," or the "recognized Cabinet," or the "regular Cabinet." However, it does not include all of the principal administrative agencies, nor do the heads of these ten departments include all of those who sit at the Cabinet table with the President. The President's Committee on Administrative Management in 1937 recommended that all administrative agencies of the government be placed under departmental supervision, with the provision that tribunals be set up for the independent exercise of quasi-judicial powers. At the same time it was recommended that two new departments be established and that all of the dozens or scores of independent operating agencies be brought under the shelter of these twelve departmental tents.

When, two years later, the Reorganization Act of 1939 was passed, the Congress forbade the President in preparing a reorganization plan to create a new department or to give anyone the title of Secretary; whereupon the President, Franklin D. Roosevelt, set up three new "agencies," not "departments," and put at the head of each an "administrator," not a "secretary." He invited the administrators of the three new agencies, the Federal Works Agency, the Federal Security Agency, and the Federal Loan Agency to sit in the Cabinet; but an administrator did not get quite as much salary as a secretary, the "regular" Cabinet members did not regard them as full members of the Cabinet, the Congress did not so regard them, and neither did the press nor the public. The indurated tradition of nomenclature proved too strong. The impact of fact had but little effect upon it.

Later, when the outbreak of World War II spurred our defense organization and, later, when we were ourselves at war, the President brought to the Cabinet table heads of principal war agencies as well, and, indeed, during the war he created one new agency, the National Housing Agency, whose administrator he invited into the Cabinet. President Truman has reduced the number of the nonregulars invited to the Cabinet, but he has not entirely excluded them.[1]

While this Cabinet is the President's principal means of operating the Executive Branch and is his principal source of official advice, it does not follow that the Cabinet always is a help. Sometimes the Cabinet hinders as well as helps. It is the President's supreme administrative task to coordinate the work of the departments and divisions of the Executive Branch. He cannot divest himself, short of virtual abdication of power, of his obligation to be manager-in-chief. Members of his Cabinet continue their jurisdictional squabbles as they have in the administration of every President. They are by no means completely willing to submit to his authority. In their resistance to the President, they do not hesitate to go to their favorite committees in Congress or to the great pressure groups with which they are in touch and many of which they consider themselves to represent, to seek aid in legal enactments, in limitations of appropriations, and in arousing public opinion. There have been times indeed when the whole Cabinet has appeared to be in a tacit conspiracy with publicists in an attempt to subvert the Constitutional authority of the Presidency and devolve it upon the Cabinet as a collegial body.

And yet, time and time again in the period of my own observation since Theodore Roosevelt was President, the opposition to the President in power, composed of a large part of the op-

---

[1] The Act of July 26, 1947, creating the National Defense Establishment has had the effect of decreasing the so-called "regular" Cabinet from ten to nine.

position party and dissident members of his own party, have bitterly complained that the President has surrounded himself with weaklings; that what he needs to do is to get a new Cabinet of strong men, thus inferring that if he could get better advice from better advisers he would change his policy.

At other times the Cabinets have been completely loyal on matters of policy, but its members prosecuted their internecine wars with what seems to be utter disregard of the additional burdens that they thus piled upon the President's back. While no President since Washington has attempted to be above party, and certainly no President since John Quincy Adams has attempted to be above politics as represented by popular political parties, every President, at least since John Quincy Adams, has selected the members of his Cabinet primarily for political reasons and only incidentally with respect to the administrative conduct of the department of which each Cabinet member is to be the head.

In choosing his Cabinet, a newly elected President—having first gained the party nomination and then won a partisan election—is subject to tremendous pressures: political, geographical, partisan, factional, as well as those arising out of the special interests of pressure groups and the personal aspirations of ambitious men. The traditions of the two parties, however, vary somewhat in this matter. Since the advent of popular participation in the elections, the Democratic Presidents, from Jackson to Franklin D. Roosevelt, have been accorded tacit permission to make their own selections. On the other hand, Whigs and Republicans have ordinarily, though not without exception, insisted that the actual choices should be made by the party leaders. Harrison and Taylor, the two Whig Presidents, resisted this domination with but partial success. Lincoln resisted but did not permit himself to resent it. Under his successor, Johnson, the Senate attempted to control the Cabinet by direct action. General Grant yielded to this pressure. President Hayes resisted it and for a considerable period of time the party leaders in control of the Senate refused to confirm any Cabinet appointment, but Hayes persisted and won the fight. Since that time even the Republican Presidents have had greater freedom. The political managers have been less demanding and the Senate has but rarely failed to confirm a nomination to a Cabinet position.

But just as Lincoln took into his Cabinet Seward, the chief of the Whigs, and Montgomery Blair, the leading Jackson Democrat, so many Presidents have sought to bring into their Cabinets other political leaders who might be expected to help prevent party splits, as in the case of Wilson in appointing William Jennings Bryan, and of Roosevelt in appointing Cordell Hull.

Then, each President in naming his Cabinet must consider geographical distribution, the relationship of such departments as Interior, Agriculture, Commerce, and Labor to specialized interests, as well as many other things. The party machinery must also be taken care of, and for decades that has taken the form of the appointment of the Chairman of the National Committee or some other practical party leader to the position of Postmaster General.

Once met around the Cabinet table the Cabinet is a council of advisers on policy. It is a council of party leaders and its members are expected to undertake individually their share of the necessary liaison work with their party colleagues in the Congress and their share of party propaganda for the general public. Then—and frequently it seems as if it were only incidental— each is expected to run his department as efficiently as possible, as quietly as possible, and in such manner as to bring up to the President as few problems as possible. Naive tyros in politics sometimes refuse to see the difficulty that confronts the President in the very nature of this team which is given to him to be his personal help. They say: "Well, if the President doesn't like a member of the Cabinet he can fire him and get another." So he can. But he must always consider whether in firing one man and hiring a successor he does not induce a greater political storm than the one which he is attempting to calm. Realistically, the President is far committed by his first choice of a Cabinet officer, and changes are difficult to make.

Members of the Cabinet are frequently strong men holding strong opinions for which they will not hesitate to fight, and if these fights lead to clashes with other members of the Cabinet their consciences as individuals constrain them to continue in their course. Each feels his responsibility to be—as indeed it is—personally to the *President* and not to the President *in council,* not to the President and his *Cabinet,* and above all not to his *Cabinet colleagues.*

The President has, it is true, the Constitutional and legal responsibility for the entire Executive Branch; but the detailed departmental organization of the Executive is controlled by the Congress, and the appropriations for the operation of the departments are made in detail by the Congress. Therefore, in these jurisdictional disputes and departmental feuds the President all too frequently finds the Cabinet, which is deemed to be his principal help, actually operating as the principal hindrance to him in carrying out his task of over-all coordination and management.

Another major hindrance in this undertaking has been the creation in recent decades of independent regulatory commissions which are considered by the Congress to be quasi-legislative and which are considered by the Courts to be quasi-judicial, and thus not being wholly a part of the Executive Branch are not subject to direct Presidential control. Yet these same independent commissions are put in charge of vast areas of administrative management over which the President has no authority but for the operation of which a realistic public opinion—and even an inconsistent Congressional opinion—continues to hold him responsible. The first of these was the Interstate Commerce Commission, which, when first established in 1887, was put in the Department of the Interior, only to be taken out and given an independent character two years later. The next was the Federal Trade Commission, set up in 1914, and since then there have been many others. Here again it seems—to me, at any rate—that tradition controls, the tradition inherent within certain Congressional committees. It is not, in my opinion, always true, as is sometimes said, that the Congress believes that a regulatory function should be entrusted to a multiheaded commission. As a matter of fact, if a proposal for a new regulatory function comes before the Interstate Commerce Committee, which is so proud of the Interstate Commerce Commission, it will bring in a bill to set up a new multiheaded commission to take care of it. If a similar matter goes before the Committee on Agriculture, so close to and so proud of the Department of Agriculture, the Committee will bring in a bill vesting that function in the Secretary of Agriculture.

Yet the public still will hold the President to the task of keeping even these independent agencies in concert with his general policies. I remember a conversation with Senator Wagner of New York, who himself was an advocate of multiheaded commissions even for ordinary administrative work, during which he admitted a point on my side and against his. He told me the story of a constituent who came to him furiously demanding that the Senator go at once to the White House and insist that the President rescind an order made by the Interstate Commerce Commission. The Senator said that he explained over and over again to his irate visitor that the ICC was independent and that the President could not give it orders. The man listened unwillingly and then at the end leaned across the desk toward the Senator, brought down his fist in a terrific blow that shook the whole office, and clinched the argument by yelling: "But the President appoints them commissioners, don't he?"

It would help the President to do his work if these independent regulatory agencies could be put under regular departments so far as all their administrative work is concerned. At the same time, without any difficulty at all, tribunals could be established for hearing and determining those quasi-judicial matters that come before the commissions.

Among the means with which we equip the President to perform his work and to meet so far as possible what we expect him to do are the staff agencies. These are relatively new in our governmental system, and being new have not acquired the traditional strength possessed by the departmental establishments. Because they are required to serve the general interest of the government and not specialized interests within it, they do not have the support of special interest groups such as those which rally behind departments and independent commissions. The first of the staff agencies was the Civil Service Commission. The reform of the Civil Service and the diminution of the evils of the partisan spoils system had its first great Presidential advocate in Rutherford B. Hayes. This movement gained great emotional support when his successor, President Garfield, was assassinated by a disappointed office seeker. Garfield's successor, President Arthur, succeeded in inducing Congress to establish the Civil Service Commission, and his successor, Grover Cleveland, in turn gave the new scheme hearty support—a support not diminished in effectiveness by his appointment of a young Republican civil service reformer as the first minority member of the Commission, Theodore Roosevelt of New York.

Since Arthur, every President of the United States without exception has by Executive Order extended the scope of the Civil

Service, despite the fact that in so doing every President has had to go directly counter to the wishes and even the demands of many of his party colleagues and often in spite of protests by members of his Cabinet. The Civil Service Commission actually was the first multiheaded commission. Its direct relationship to the President as a staff agency was not recognized and it probably became the precedent which led to the establishment of the Interstate Commerce Commission independent of departmental control. The essential staff character of the Civil Service Commission, however, was inherent in its very nature. It was intended to serve all the departments, the rules that it was to enforce were to be issued only by the President, and every President always has had the power with one stroke of the pen to abolish the entire Civil Service system by simply exempting all positions from its operations.

The next landmark in providing staff help for the President was the passage in 1921 of the Budget and Accounting Act. This provided for the first time that an Executive budget be submitted to the Congress by the President; it set up a Bureau of the Budget to help the President prepare that Executive budget, and it established a General Accounting Office. The Bureau of the Budget, it is true, was located in the Treasury Department, and the General Accounting Office was created as an agent of the Congress without any clear lines of responsibility. At the same time, while the number of appropriation bills was reduced and the consideration of the budget devolved in each House upon a single Appropriations Committee (instead of being scattered amongst ten or a dozen separate committees), the Act fell short of the requirements of the situation. That it did fall short was due not only to the necessary elements of compromise inescapable in the legislative process, but also to the fact that the problem was not at that time clearly understood. Had the creation of the single Executive budget been accompanied by a requirement for a single appropriation bill much more would have been accomplished. Yet it must be said that the passage of this act in 1921 gave the President a greater measure of effective control over the Cabinet departments, and to a degree even over the independent establishments, than ever before had been enjoyed by any head of the Executive Branch.

The next addition to the equipment of the President for performing his task was the creation of the Executive Office of the President, under authority of the Reorganization Act of 1939. In this Office were placed, at the beginning, the White House Office itself, the Bureau of the Budget, the National Resources Planning Board, the Office of Government Reports, and the Office for Emergency Management.

The Presidency had been in existence for 150 years, but not until the summer of 1939 was there an Executive Office of the President; nor did the President have immediately under his supervision any more than a very small and inadequate secretarial and clerical force. Indeed, either because Presidents were unwilling to ask for the necessary appropriations or Congress was unwilling to grant them, the White House had to depend for its clerical force for the most part upon clerks assigned to it from other departments. I remember asking one of these men in the White House, when Theodore Roosevelt was President, how long he had been there. He astonished me by saying that he *never* had been there, but was still a clerk in the Department of Agriculture. He stayed on the payroll of the Department of Agriculture until he was retired for old age, but he worked in the White House under every President from McKinley to Franklin D. Roosevelt.

The White House staff was headed by a single secretary until Mr. Hoover changed the custom by appointing three secretaries, a custom followed by Mr. Roosevelt, although the apportionment of duties among the three varied from time to time.

The President's Committee on Administrative Management in its report in 1937 had pointed out that the President needed help. It recommended that he be given six administrative assistants, and at the same time it recommended that the President should "have at his command a contingent fund to enable him to bring in from time to time particular persons possessed of particular competency for a particular purpose and whose services he might usefully employ for short periods of time." The Congress denied the President any such fund but gave him the six executive assistants, many of whom have been used for the purposes envisaged by the second recommendation. In the original conception of their roles, these assistants were to be characterized by a "passion for anonymity," and since I must plead guilty to the charge of being responsible for this frightful phrase which has fastened on to these assistants, I hope I may be pardoned for a digression while I relate its origin.

The President's Committee had asked Professor Lindsay Rogers of Columbia University to prepare a report on the organization and procedures of the British and French Cabinet secretariats. I was myself in the summer of 1936 in London and sought to see Sir Maurice Hankey, then the head of the British Cabinet secretariat. He was not in London, but I did find Tom Jones, a man whom I had known for many years and who had served as secretary to at least three Prime Ministers—Lloyd George, MacDonald, and Baldwin—and who was himself Sir Maurice's deputy. He told me that he thought I should tell President Roosevelt that the thing to do was to adjust the model of the British Cabinet secretariat to fit the Presidential rather than the parliamentary system and then to get one man to head it. "A man," he said, "like Hankey, a man of high competence, great physical vigor, and a passion for anonymity." Later, in our conversations with the President, the members of the Committee, Dr. Merriam, Dr. Gulick, and I, found Mr. Roosevelt reluctant to set up any sort of secretariat under one person. After hearing him at length we agreed with him, and thus came to recommend a corps of administrative assistants instead of an administrative secretariat under a single head. At the same time we expressly recommended that they would be in addition to his three secretaries. It was at that time the President's expressed intention to consider one of them as *primus inter pares,* or as he expressed it, "One of them will stay here in the office and help me keep track of them all."

The President's Committee has been severely criticized by Professor Lindsay Rogers and others for yielding this point to President Roosevelt, it being Mr. Rogers' contention that such a committee should have made up its own recommendations, put them on the President's table, and left to the President the responsibility for changes. This happens not to have been the conception of the task that the members of the Committee entertained. We had been appointed to an official committee by the President and we thought we should consult him, especially about his own office, inclining to the notion that he might know more about the Presidency than any or all of us. And finally, Professor Rogers does not seem to have taken into consideration the possibility that perhaps the President persuaded us to his own view.

From the moment that the President, in the special press conference in which he gave out for publication the report of our Committee, paused at what he called that "purple patch" about the administrative assistants and read it with deliberate emphasis, "sky blue ruin began a'brewin' for the luckless" persons who were to have those jobs. There was instant journalistic laughter and disbelief that a person with such a passion did exist. It made no difference that the President immediately responded to the laugh by pointing out that here was Rudolph Forster who had been pursuing anonymity in the White House for nigh onto forty years. The troublesome label stuck. My contrition cannot cure the hurt.

The White House secretariat still requires, in my opinion, a better organization, and the President has not been sufficiently equipped in his own office with the help necessary for him to do his work. I say this with no intention of derogating from the importance of the establishment of the Executive Office of the President. By that establishment the equipment of the President was advantaged in several important ways. First in order of importance, perhaps, was taking the Bureau of the Budget out of the Treasury, placing it directly under the President, and expanding the scope of its activities. This is not the place to undertake a detailed description of the Bureau of the Budget. Let me simply say that since its transfer to the Executive Office, the President has used it successfully as a tool for the coordination of the many departments and divisions of the Executive Branch, not only with respect to estimates for appropriations and other fiscal matters, but also with increasing efficiency as an engine to aid him in coordinating general legislative programs and the work of administrative management of the entire government.

As I have indicated in a previous lecture, the National Resources Planning Board, which was most useful in its help to the President, was abolished by the Congress on what seemed to be the general theory that it was indulging in the sinful practice of economic planning. Since then Congress has set up a Council of Economic Advisers whose planning activities are more or less limited to economic planning, and has placed this Council in the Executive Office of the President.

The plan setting up the Executive Office of the President, which was approved by both Houses of the Congress, also authorized the President to provide an Office for Emergency Management. This he did on September 8, 1939, seven days after Hitler invaded Poland and started World War II. The Office for Emergency Management was not conceived primarily as an operating agency. Rather, it was a scheme to give the President a certain administrative flexibility roughly comparable to that afforded corporate management by the device of a holding company. During the defense period, and later even after Pearl Harbor had brought us into the war, the OEM was used by the President to house and foster the growth of literally dozens of defense and war agencies. Had Roosevelt been forced, like Wilson, to go to the Congress for a statutory enactment in support of every new defense or war agency, the defense and war efforts would have been delayed and perhaps sometimes defeated. There was a further benefit to be enjoyed from this arrangement as against a statutory basis to the war agencies: if a change were deemed desirable, the whole legislative process would have had to be invoked, in the case of agencies supported by legislative enactments, whereas under OEM the President could try out a certain device and if it did not work, as frequently it did not, he could abolish it and set up another. When the history of our period comes to be written, I have no doubt that the verdict will be that the President was greatly aided in his tremendous task of coordinating the diverse elements involved in the mobilization of the national resources for a total war by this device of the Office for Emergency Management.

In addition to the formalized equipment available to the President as represented in the members of the Cabinet and the heads of the independent administrative agencies, and of the staff agencies grouped within the Executive Office of the President, he has also available various informal aids. One, of course, is the party, through which the President keeps in touch with the members of Congress who belong to his party and with the party leaders and managers. Another is the machinery, the exact form of which varies with every President, by which he keeps in touch with members of the Congress.

Far more important, however, is that informal group of friends who have access to the President and upon whom he relies for information, advice, and sometimes perhaps for admonition. Mr. Jonathan Daniels, in his book *Frontier on the Potomac,* writing out of his own experience as a member of the White House secretariat, discusses this matter in a chapter entitled "The Palace Guard." In my opinion, Mr. Daniels is quite right when he says that every President must have immediately about him both experts and intimates. Whether he is right or not, practically all Presidents seem to have thought so. At any rate, most of them have had their intimates, and in recent times, with the growing size and complexity of the executive establishment, they have had their experts as well. The experts are governmental and official. The intimates are personal and unofficial. From the day of Andrew Jackson and his Kitchen Cabinet until today every President has been under fire because of them. Some Presidents, Grant and Harding conspicuously, suffered betrayal at their hands, but it seems that no President can do without them and many have benefited greatly because of them.

These Presidential intimates, however, are always the objects of jealousy and intrigue, and because of their very unofficial character are the targets of scathing criticism from the suspicious and the cynical. Few perhaps have attained that eminence of intimacy typified by Colonel House and Harry Hopkins. Some perhaps have managed to preserve a considerable degree of anonymity, but they have been there and will continue to be there.

The greatest factor in the tragedy of the Presidency is perhaps its awful loneliness. The lofty eminence to which we lift on election day every four years the man of our choice cuts him off from normal and usual contacts with his fellow men. The immense burden of his office, despite every aid that we have yet been able or willing to give him, accentuates his isolation. His stature as the symbol of the State invests him with an awe that keeps most of his fellows at a distance. Whether as individual Americans we like him or not, whether we approve of him or not, whether we deprecate him or not, even if, as we sometimes do, we actually hate him, we still are constrained to respect his office and to yield ceremonial respect to his person. When political enemies fail to yield this meed of respect to the President we are apt to condemn them for carrying their personal opposition to the President over into disrespect for the Presidency.

It follows, then, that if the President is not to permit himself to be shut up as a prisoner in the White House he must maintain some channels of communication that are not formal and official, some way of reaching out into the country to discover what people are thinking about events and about his manner of dealing with them. He cannot be denied this help.

One President, Franklin D. Roosevelt, found his help at home in Mrs. Roosevelt, who with a minimum of ceremony and with a maximum of energy kept in touch with thousands and thousands of her fellow citizens and was eyes and ears for her husband. Other Presidents have found other ways in which to mitigate the evils of the loneliness of eminence. Naturally some have been more successful than others. In this, as in so many other things, does the Presidency depend upon the man who is the President.

While we are considering the equipment that we have given the Presidency for the performance of its tasks, we should not block out of our minds how we handle it. We vest the executive power in a President of the United States of America and then we hamper him by withholding from him authority commensurate with that responsibility. We expect him to lead us and we put stumbling blocks and build barriers across the way. We expect him to obey us and we deprive him of the power to do so. Of such elements are compounded many of the failures which we charge to our Presidents. Out of such little lacks on our part are compounded the great lacks of the President. We crush him beneath the burdens of our requirements and refuse him the help that he needs to carry them. For every variance from the course we demand he take we denounce him. If he fails to act we call him a weakling. If he does act we call him a dictator. We esteem him as the Chief of State and we despise him as a time-serving politician. We ask him to dignify our celebrations by his presence, and we whisper vile slanders about him and impute to him both malevolence and corruption.

But we will again next year, as we have in the past and as we shall probably do quadrennially in the future, choose a mere man to be President and then endow him with the care and responsibility of the Presidency. As time goes on we shall probably depend upon him even more than we have in the past to be our principal servant. We may even persuade ourselves to give him the tools he needs if he is to do what we want him to do: to manage the government; to engineer the national economy; to reflect our opinions as Americans; and to lead the nation— even to lead the world.

[VI]

What Help Does the President Need from Us?

THE PEOPLE OF THE United States in 1787 ordained, among other things, that "The executive Power shall be vested in a President of the United States of America." Two years later, when that ordinance had been ratified by eleven of the then thirteen states of the Union, the first President took office and assumed the burden of the Presidency. In the 160 years that have intervened there have been many changes. What was a weak confederation of thirteen independent and sovereign states, having together only little more than three million people scattered along the eastern seaboard, and with barely enough faith in their national future to undertake the experiment of the new Constitution, has changed into a strong nation of fifty times that number of people, belting the North American continent from ocean to ocean, sobered by the awakening realization of its responsibilities as leader of the world, but yet confidently content with that same Constitution which endures without essential change.

Then, in 1787, the youngest nation in the world and a republic in a world in which republics were rare, now, in 1947, it is with perhaps but one exception constitutionally the oldest nation and the first republic in a world in which republics are the rule. Moreover, the distinction between monarchy and republic, then so sharp and so significant, is all but forgotten today in the debates that fill the air about the distinctions between democracy and totalitarianism, between capitalism and communism, and the even more furious dispute concerning the very meaning of the word "democracy" which is claimed as the exclusive sign manual of two very different sets of political systems.

However, the changes that have been made in the Constitution of 1787, although not affecting essentially its form and structure, have been chiefly in the direction of democratization (using that word in its Western sense), whether those changes have been formal amendments to the Constitution itself or the result of the accretion of accepted usage and common consent.

For our first President we chose George Washington because by common consent he was the leader of the nation. From his successors we have expected leadership, and we have placed the names of those Presidents who did most to meet that expectation on the roster of great Presidents.

At the same time as we vested the executive power in a President, we vested the legislative power (over such concerns as we did not reserve to the states and to the people) in a Congress of the United States, and we vested the judicial power "in one supreme Court." This separation of powers so neatly and tersely written down by us as a people in 1787 has not, of course, prevented profound differences of opinion with respect to the boundaries of their several provinces; on the contrary it has given rise to intense rivalry that has manifested itself, among other ways, in billions of words of debate. At this time I am accepting without question the assumption that the people were right 160 years ago in separating the powers, and that they have been and are now right in retaining that separation.

Certainly this is not the place nor am I the person even so much as to attempt to review, much less resolve, that sixteen-decade, billion-word debate. Rather I have attempted in these talks to focus attention upon one of the separated powers—the Executive. I have tried to talk only about the President and the Presidency in relation to what "We, the people" have ordained, and to discuss the nature of our present relationship to this high office which we have endowed with the executive power and in which we place every four years a man of our own choosing.

In the preceding lecture I have briefly sketched the structural equipment we have given the Presidency to enable it to perform the tasks we have imposed upon it. I have indicated that in my opinion this equipment is inadequate. Therefore, I conclude, the President needs help. He can get the help that he needs only from us, the people. What action, then, should we take to mend this situation? We should, in my opinion, do two things. First, we should give the President authority commensurate with his responsibility—something that we have not done. Second, we should hold him to strict accountability for the exercise of that authority—something that we have not done.

The steps that we should take to do these two things are various. Some of them are negative and require us to remove the shackles we have already placed upon his authority and refrain in the future from further hampering his action. Some of them are positive and require us to contrive better machinery for the administration of the Presidency and new and better means for holding the President to stricter accountability.

When I say, as I have said several times in these lectures, that we should give the President authority commensurate with his responsibility, I do not mean that he should be given additional power. He already has the power. What he needs is *authority* to exercise it effectively.

"Authority," in this sense, does not mean power to spend money. The power of the purse is in the Congress and no money can be drawn from the Treasury unless it has been appropriated by law. Nor does it mean power over persons or property. Powers affecting men and their goods have been entrusted by the people to the Congress of the United States or have been reserved to the states or the people.

Such authority does not mean power to transcend the law or the Constitution; it does not mean power to invade public or private rights; nor does it mean one-man rule or dictatorship or the destruction of democracy, or anything in the slightest manner faintly resembling totalitarianism. But such authority does mean that the Presidency be enabled to carry out its constitutional mandate and that the President be authorized, without hindrance, to do the things required of him by the Constitution; the things that we the people require of him.

A first constructive step in this direction would be to permit a continuous process of reorganization of the Executive Branch so as to meet the ever-changing needs of administrative management.

Acting through the Congress, we should see to it that all the administrative agencies of the federal government be grouped in a manageable number of major departments, each under the direction of a principal officer appointed by the President and subject, of course, to confirmation by the Senate. Then the President should be given authority to reorganize and regroup the divisions and bureaus and to redistribute the functions within any one of the great departments by means of an Executive Order. Then the precedents of the Reorganization Acts of 1939 and 1945 should be followed by the enactment of a permanent Reorganization Act, stripped of all exemptions and limitations. Under such a law, the President would be authorized at his discretion to submit to the Congress from time to time particular reorganization plans that might involve more than one great department, which plans, unless disapproved by the legislative veto as set out in the Reorganization Acts of 1939 and 1945, would become law. If these two steps were taken, the Executive Branch, acting within the law and subject in major matters to the legislative veto, might over a period of twenty or thirty years carefully, cautiously, and prudently trim away the vast procedural jungle-growth that now impedes efficient operation and makes a mockery of true economy.

The next step which we the people should take to meet the needs of the Presidency is to persuade the Congress not to yield to the constant temptation to interfere with the administration of the Executive Branch by needlessly detailed requirements for procedures in the execution of the laws it enacts; procedures sometimes so hampering that they almost have the effect of defeating the very purpose for which the Congress has enacted the law. The President is under the Constitutional obligation to "take Care that the Laws be faithfully executed," and if we mean to help the President to discharge this obligation we must be sure that his authority so to do is not usurped either by the Congress as a whole, by the House of Representatives or the Senate, and—most important of all—by particular committees of the Congress.

At one time in the history of the Republic, the usurpation of the executive power by Congressional committees constituted so great an encroachment upon the executive power that the President was all but overwhelmed. A description of that state of affairs is available to us in Woodrow Wilson's classic, *Congressional Government*. It is true, as I have indicated elsewhere, that long before Mr. Wilson became President he recognized that the Presidency was being restored to its Constitutional status. But there never has been a time when little invasions have not been made by Congressional committees and subcommittees and even mere committee chairmen, often in what amounts to a conspiratorial concert with Presidential subordinates, most frequently in the dark and but rarely subjected to the light of that "pitiless publicity" which Woodrow Wilson said illuminated the Presidency.

What the Congress should retain, what the Congress must retain, what the Congress cannot abdicate, is the power of the purse. To the extent that laws enacted in pursuance of the Constitution require appropriations, these funds must be voted by the Congress or they cannot be withdrawn from the Treasury. The Congress annually, therefore, has the opportunity to review, when it passes upon the President's budget, the whole vast machinery of the government. Under these circumstances no President could long usurp powers not legally his.

On the other side, it is for the people to see to it that the Congress stops the practice of using appropriation measures as a vehicle for writing into law things that otherwise would meet with the Presidential veto, which would not command sufficient support to be passed over that veto, and which, in many cases, could not otherwise gain the support of even a majority of the two Houses. Not only should the Congress cease the vicious practice of attaching legislative riders to appropriation bills, which it does in violation of its own rules, but it also should cease to attach to specific appropriations specific procedural limitations that will have the effect of impeding the equitable administration of the very law for the execution of which the appropriation ostensibly is granted.

The President should be given adequate power to repel these petty usurpations, each of which in itself may seem to amount to but little, but which, taken together over long periods of time, effectively vitiate the authority of the President over his subordinates in the Executive Branch. Members of the British government from time to time are heard to complain of the predominant position of the Treasury over other departments.[1] It was Léon Blum who remarked that the mastery by the Treasury in the British governmental system had been attained by means of a "long and happy series of usurpations."[2]

[1] *Thoughts on the Constitution,* by L. S. Amery. London: Oxford University Press, 1947, p. 94.

[2] "La réforme que je propose revient en somme à ceci: conférer à la Présidence du Conseil, en matière d'administration et de législation générale, de pouvoirs analogues

It was by such a series of usurpations that so-called Congressional government—government by standing committees of the Congress—all but reduced the Presidency to what Grover Cleveland might have called innocuous desuetude during the years between the Civil War and the Spanish War. Indeed, the evil was sensed and recognized even before the Civil War during the period of the weak presidents—*les rois fainéants*—that intervened between Polk and Lincoln. Oddly enough, the evidence of the early discovery of this particular weakness of the American Executive is to be found in the Constitution of the Confederate States of America. That Constitution did endow the Presidency with means to repel such petty usurpations. It gave the President the power to veto specific items in appropriation bills.

We should today give the President of the United States this same power of veto over specific items in the supply bills. Without this power, the President often feels compelled to sign supply bills despite their freight of obnoxious items and legislative riders rather than risk the stoppage of whole governmental departments for want of funds. Not infrequently the President feels impelled to announce to the public that he has signed an appropriation bill with reluctance because it contained specific items which he deemed bad, but which he could not veto without vetoing the entire measure.

To give the President this power of item veto would not make him a "dictator." It would help him more faithfully to reflect the will of the people. And, of course, if he misused the power, the item could be repassed over his objection if it could muster a two-thirds vote in both houses of the Congress, just as if he vetoes an entire bill.

à ceux que le Ministère des Finances c'est acquis, par une longue et heureuse suite d'usurpations, sur tout ce qui touche les dépenses publiques." *La Réforme Gouvernementale,* by Léon Blum. Paris: Bernard Grasset, 1936, p. 62.

If this proposed grant of authority to the President is objected to because it is too great to fit in with the American way of life, or because it had its origin in the Constitution of the Confederate States of America—which certainly, even if unsuccessfully, advocated the overthrow of our government by force—a view of the Constitutions of the various states in the Union may provide some reassurance.

In no fewer than 39 of the 48 states of the Union the people have given the Governor of the state this power to veto specific items in appropriation bills. In some of them this power has been extended so that the Governor may approve, disapprove, or modify specific items. The movement to give this power to the American Executive, as represented in the Governors, began in 1865 when Georgia adopted it from the then defunct Confederate Constitution. Texas did the same thing in 1866. The movement gathered force but slowly until the period of state reorganization beginning just after the turn of the century. The power of the item veto now is vested in the Governors of all the states with the exception of Indiana, Iowa, Maine, Nevada, New Hampshire, North Carolina (the only state in which the Governor has no veto power over bills), Rhode Island, Tennessee, and Vermont.

Some Constitutional lawyers in and out of Congress have held that the essential power of item veto may be given to the President by Act of Congress without an amendment to the Constitution. Certainly such a self-denying ordinance by the Congress would be more expeditious than the amendatory process. In my opinion, we the people should endeavor to persuade our Senators and Representatives to take action; if possible by law, if not, then by the submission of an amendment to the Constitution, that would give the President the power of item veto now granted to most state Governors. Such a process would leave the Presidency with sufficient authority to meet its Constitutional obligations; with sufficient authority, subject always to the Constitution and the laws and subject always to the legislative control of the purse, to meet its responsibilities to the people.

We must, however, acknowledge the fact that many of the hampering Congressional acts which have interfered with even the most minute details of administration have come about because we have not yet established any means by which we can hold the President to strict accountability for his acts and especially for the expenditure of the funds granted him by the Congress. Mr. Lucius Wilmerding in his book, *The Spending Power,* has painted a rather dismal picture of the unavailing efforts made by the Congress, from the very beginning, to exercise efficient supervision over the expenditure of the funds it has appropriated. One such effort was made in the Budget and Accounting Act of 1921 when the General Accounting Office was set up. The Comptroller General at the head of that office is described in the statute as the agent of the Congress, but there is no means by which the principal may control the day-to-day operations of its agent.

The President's Committee on Administrative Management in 1937 attempted to deal with this problem. In its original recommendation, the President's Committee, being persuaded that it was a legal necessity, provided for the appointment of an Auditor General, by the President, who would be required to report his transactions continuously to a Joint Committee on Accounts of the Congress. Later, the President's Committee recommended to the Joint Congressional Committee set up to consider its report that the Auditor General be appointed by the Congress itself. The report of the President's Committee came before the Joint Congressional Committee and the public at the time when the whole country was in a furor over President Roosevelt's recommendations for a change in the constitution of the Supreme Court. At the same time, the President's Committee was compelled, again under advice of counsel, to use the phrase "abolish the Comptroller General" as a condition prerequisite to establishing the Auditor General. The whole business became involved in a confusion of technical accounting terms employed quite frequently by persons who were not technicians and who did not know the meaning of the terms they used. I fear that it will take much time and great patience for us, through our representatives in Congress, to clear away the debris left by that debate and induce the Congress to take steps to make the President, and through him, the entire Executive Branch, actually accountable through the whole range of its fiscal activities. This matter was thus set up in the report made by the President's Committee on January 8, 1937: [3]

We have called attention to this difficulty with respect to fiscal accountability. We hold that once the Congress has made an appropriation, an appropriation which it is free to withhold, the responsibility for the administration of the expenditures under that appropriation is and should be solely upon the Executive.

The Executive then should be held to account through an independent audit made by an independent auditor who will report promptly to the Congress his criticisms and exceptions of the actions of the Executive. Based upon these reports the approoriate committees of the Congress may call upon an executive officer to explain his conduct and if it has been characterized by illegality or impropriety, the Congress can take the necessary corrective steps and safeguard the future.

With respect to the accountability of the Executive Branch to the Legislative Branch for fiscal and other activities, the difficulty now is that the diffusion and dispersion of activities in the uncoordinated organization of the Executive Branch is twinned by a similar diffusion and dispersion in the Congress. Separate committees of the Congress must of necessity be set up to pursue investigatorial activities, hold hearings, and consider legislation and appropriations.

[3] *Administrative Management in the Government of the United States:* Report of the President's Committee on Administrative Management. Washington: Government Printing Office, 1937.

But the Congress has not in either House adequate machinery for the collection and coordination of the information which it requires if it is to hold the President effectively accountable for the conduct of the Executive Branch as a whole.

With respect to fiscal affairs this need might be met by the organization by each House of special committees or by both Houses of a joint committee on fiscal control to receive the reports of its Auditor General.

With respect to nonfiscal affairs, the creation of similar special committees or of a joint committee to keep currently informed of the activities of the three managerial agencies dealing with budget, personnel, and planning, which we recommend should be set up directly under the President, would go far toward lessening the evil effects of the present lack of coordination.

Thus the principle of the accountability of the Executive to the Congress might be made effective in action.

The failure thus far to take the necessary steps to hold the President to strict accountability to the Congress for the administration of the funds voted by it to the Executive Branch and the laws passed by it for the governance of the nation cannot be charged to the President or the Presidency. At various times and in various ways Presidents Theodore Roosevelt, William Howard Taft, Woodrow Wilson, and Herbert Hoover attempted to deal with the problem; and in his message to Congress of January 12, 1937, transmitting the report of the President's Committee, President Franklin D. Roosevelt expressly approved this recommendation for strict accountability of the Executive Branch.

Some progress toward this goal of accountability is being made in the Legislative Branch by such devices as the setting up of the Joint Committee on Atomic Energy and the increased use of joint committees for maintaining current contact with the Executive Branch with respect to planning and the conduct of particular policy programs. In the field of foreign affairs, a notable advance in cooperation between the President and the Senate was brought about through the establishment by Secretary of State Cordell Hull of a system of informal conversations with the members of the Foreign Affairs Committee of the Senate. This practice has since been resumed from time to time, and bids fair to enable the United States better to pursue a consistent foreign policy; and it can do so without, on the one hand, usurping the Constitutional initiative of the President, or, on the other hand, prejudicing the joint responsibility of the Senate, which, so far as the ratification of treaties is concerned, acts as a part of the Executive Branch.

Another thing that we the people can do to meet the needs of the President so as to enable him the better to fulfill his responsibilities to us, is to give him authority over his own office; or if he already has sufficient authority (and I think perhaps he has for all immediate and practical purposes), to assure him that we will back him up if he uses it.

In this connection it is necessary for us, I think, to remember that the failure of a President to live up to those of our expectations as are legally possible is not all the fault of the Congress, or of the Court, or of the party, or of the people. Sometimes it is the fault of the President himself. Some Presidents have shrunk from assuming the responsibility even within the scope of their authority. It would perhaps be neither quite accurate nor quite fair to say that Mr. Coolidge deliberately abdicated his power. At the same time it is true, I think, that his concept of the position he held was such that he carried the principle of delegation to such an extreme that it amounted in fact to abdication. In his time, Mr. Mellon in the Treasury and Senator Smoot on the Hill between them managed the administrative machinery of the government. It was a quiet time and during the seven-and-a-half years Mr. Coolidge was in the White House no great crisis occurred to bring his peculiar notions of administration into the forefront of the national consciousness. It is, indeed, quite possible that had there been a crisis Mr. Coolidge would have taken over the helm to meet it.

As I say, it was a quiet time. People in town were busy, stocks were going up, and while there was discontent down on the farm and the storm clouds were gathering, for the most part everything was serene. The people, or most of them (except perhaps the farmers, who were just finding their collective voice) did not want the President to do anything, and Calvin Coolidge met their expectations.

Only recently I happened to talk with Mr. John W. Davis, who was the unsuccessful candidate against Mr. Coolidge in the Presidential election of 1924. In a reminiscent mood Mr. Davis was ranging over the electoral contests for the Presidency since McKinley's defeat of Bryan. He concluded with this: "Well, one thing is pretty sure. The people usually know what they want at a particular time, and they usually know how to get it at the polls. Certainly in 1924 when I was a candidate what they wanted was repose. They voted for it. They got it. I would not have given it to them."

However we may classify the Coolidge episode, it nevertheless remains true that we the people have demanded action of every other President since McKinley. The type of action that we have got in response to that demand of course has varied with the personality of the President. Earlier in these lectures I quoted the sarcastic riposte of President Taft to Theodore Roosevelt's division of the Presidents into two classes, the Buchanan type and the Lincoln type. What Mr. Roosevelt was saying was that some Presidents had a narrow view of their authority, a view narrowed by legalistic and literalistic interpretation of the Constitution, while other Presidents with equal sincerity took the broad view. Also, and here he was talking particularly about Mr. Taft, Theodore Roosevelt said that some Presidents did not employ the authority which they unquestionably possessed, but preferred rather to pass on to some other agency the determination of their difficult problems. In his *Autobiography,* Mr. Roosevelt said:[4]

As to all action of this kind there have long been two schools of political thought, upheld with equal sincerity. The division has not normally been along political, but temperamental, lines. The course I followed, of regarding the executive as subject only to the people, and, under the Constitution, bound to serve the people affirmatively in cases where the Constitution does not explicitly forbid him to render the service, was substantially the course followed by both Andrew Jackson and Abraham Lincoln. Other honorable and well-meaning Presidents, such as James Buchanan, took the opposite and, as it seems to me, narrowly legalistic view that the President is the servant of Congress rather than of the people, and can do nothing, no matter how necessary it be to act, unless the Constitution explicitly commands the action. Most able lawyers who are past middle age take this view, and so do large numbers of well-meaning, respectable citizens. My successor in office took this, the Buchanan, view of the President's powers and duties.

. . . . .

Perhaps the sharp difference between what may be called the Lincoln-Jackson and the Buchanan-Taft schools, in their views of the power and duties of the President, may be best illustrated by comparing the attitude of my successor toward his Secretary of the Interior, Mr. Ballinger, when the latter was accused of gross misconduct in office, with my attitude towards my chiefs of departments and other subordinate officers. More than once while I was President my officials were attacked by Congress, generally because these officials did their duty well and fearlessly. In every such case I stood by the official and refused to recognize the right of Congress to interfere with me excepting by impeachment or in other Constitutional manner. On the other hand, wherever I found the officer unfit for his position I promptly removed him, even although the most influential men in Congress fought for his retention. The Jackson-

---

[4] *Theodore Roosevelt: An Autobiography.* New York: Charles Scribner's Sons, 1913, p. 362 ff.

Lincoln view is that a President who is fit to do good work should be able to form his own judgment as to his own subordinates, and, above all, of the subordinates standing highest and in closest and most intimate touch with him. My secretaries and their subordinates were responsible to me, and I accepted the responsibility for all their deeds. As long as they were satisfactory to me I stood by them against every critic or assailant, within or without Congress; and as for getting Congress to make up my mind for me about them, the thought would have been inconceivable to me. My successor took the opposite, or Buchanan, view when he permitted and requested Congress to pass judgment on the charges made against Mr. Ballinger as an executive officer. These charges were made to the President; the President had the facts before him and could get at them at any time, and he alone had power to act if the charges were true. However, he permitted and requested Congress to investigate Mr. Ballinger. The party minority of the committee that investigated him, and one member of the majority, declared that the charges were well founded and that Mr. Ballinger should be removed. The other members of the majority declared the charges ill founded. The President abode by the view of the majority. Of course believers in the Jackson-Lincoln theory of the Presidency would not be content with this town meeting majority and minority method of determining by another branch of the Government what it seems the especial duty of the President himself to determine for himself in dealing with his own subordinate in his own department.

There are many worthy people who reprobate the Buchanan method as a matter of history, but who in actual life reprobate still more strongly the Jackson-Lincoln method when it is put into practice. These persons conscientiously believe that the President should solve every doubt in favor of inaction as against action, that he should construe strictly and narrowly the Constitutional grant of powers both to the National Government, and to the President within the National Government. In addition, however, to the men who conscientiously believe in this course from high, although as I hold misguided, motives, there are many men who affect to believe in it merely because it enables them to attack and to try to hamper, for partisan or personal reasons, an executive whom they dislike. There are other men in whom, especially when they are themselves in office, practical adherence to the Buchanan principle represents not well-thought-out devotion to an unwise course, but simple weakness of character and desire to avoid trouble and responsibility. Unfortunately, in practice it makes little difference which class of ideas actuates the President, who by his action sets a cramping precedent. Whether he is highminded and wrongheaded or merely infirm of purpose, whether he means well feebly or is bound by a mischievous misconception of the powers and duties of the National Government and of the President, the effect of his actions is the same. The President's duty is to act so that he himself and his subordinates shall be able to do efficient work for the people, and this efficient work he and they cannot do if Congress is permitted to undertake the task of making up his mind for him as to how he shall perform what is clearly his sole duty.

However, whether a President in all sincerity takes the narrow or the broad view of his responsibilities, he cannot lessen the range of the demands made upon him, nor can he ever meet all expectations. The expectations themselves are contradictory. Those who opposed his election will not be so bitter as those who supported him if disappointment comes, because the opponents naturally have little faith in their own expectations. Considering that what he does concerns so many things and is compounded in the presence of the complex activities over which he presides, the most any President can do perhaps is to meet the expectations of a little more than a majority of all the people.

After all these qualifications are taken into consideration, I think it is fair to say that Presidents who exercise to the full their authority for leadership occasion fewer and less poignant disappointments than do those Presidents who, because of conviction or otherwise, refrain from exercising the full powers of their office. That is why in the period about which I have been talking the names of Theodore Roosevelt, Woodrow Wilson, and Franklin Delano Roosevelt stand out so prominently. But whether the President is either "strong" or "weak" in the largest view of his function, short of abdication he cannot divest himself of responsibility for coordinating the program and policy of the Executive Branch of the government. Even if he attempts to exercise the coordinating function by delegation, still he must retain some measure of control and still he must have some means of knowing what has been done with the authority he has delegated. To that end, as I said before, we must support the President. More than that, we should even demand of him that he so organize his own Presidential office that we can have a reasonable assurance that the national program and the national policy—which is our program and our policy—be consistent and not contradictory, be capable of administration with efficiency and economy, and be attuned to what we tell him we want him to do.

It will not do to create a Deputy President, or an Assistant President, or any Cabinet secretariat on the so-called British model that will stand between the President and his subordinates. It will not do to make of the Vice President a so-called "Operating Vice President" in charge of the administrative machinery. Much as has been said of the burdens of the Presidency, it still remains clear that to divide its responsibility amongst others would multiply, not reduce, those burdens. The principle of unity of command is as valid in the Executive Branch of the government as it is in the military, and indeed in our system the two are combined at the top. The President is Manager-in-Chief of the Executive Branch just as he is Commander-in-Chief of the Armed Forces of the nation.

If the President is to retain his right to work through his own secretariat when he chooses, or through his managerial staff agencies when he chooses, or through department heads either singly or in combination as he chooses—a right essential to the protection of his Constitutional position—he should, in my opinion reject any proposal for a "Deputy President" or "Assistant President." And he should also, in my opinion, reject the proposal (recurrently made) for a "Cabinet secretariat" on the so-called British model.

Most of the administrative work of the government is done through the department heads who collectively compose the Cabinet. All of it should be done through them, I think, and all administrative activities, now scattered among the so-called "independent agencies" should be transferred to executive departments. But the departments and the department heads must be subordinate to the President. Either singly, or in groups, or collectively as the Cabinet, they are the President's creatures and should be subject to him. Of course he will take their advice but he cannot, short of virtual abdication, subject himself to their decisions.

Mr. Burton J. Hendrick in his recent book, *Lincoln's War Cabinet,* has illuminated for us the enormous political and practical problems of a President in dealing with a Cabinet in which more than one member did not regard himself as a subordinate of the President. Since the emergence of the modern phase of the Presidency, beginning with Theodore Roosevelt, all Presidents have faced similar problems in greater or less degree. If at any juncture during this period the Cabinet had been institutionalized by the device of a Cabinet secretariat, I for one believe that the troubles would have been multiplied.

Indeed, the British model may not be all that it is cracked up to be, even when related to a parliamentary system. I am persuaded that it could not be grafted onto the Presidential system. In this opinion I am bolstered by a distinguished English witness. Mr. L. S. Amery, who in one way or another, as a private secretary, member of the House of Commons, and member of several Cabinets, has had fifty years of experience with the British parliamentary system, recently distilled the fruits of his labor and observation in a series of four lectures at Oxford. Published as a small book under the title, *Thoughts on the Constitution,* Mr. Amery's comments on the British Cabinet and its workings are not without great value for us Americans as well as for the Britons to whom they are addressed. Perhaps Presidents and Prime Ministers are more akin than some of us have thought, but it is obvious that Cabinet Ministers in Britain and department heads in the United States, meeting in their respective Cabinets, are sisters under the skin. Says Mr. Amery: [5]

. . . I cannot do better than repeat to-day what I wrote more than ten years ago about the way in which the normal Cabinet system works:*

'We attempt to direct the affairs of a great nation by weekly meetings between departmental chiefs, all absorbed in the routine of their departments, all concerned to secure Cabinet sanction for this or that departmental proposal, all giving a purely temporary and more or less perfunctory attention to the issues brought up by other departments. Every Cabinet meeting is a scramble to get through the agenda in which the competition of departments for a place is varied by the incursion of urgent telegrams from abroad or of sudden questions in the House of Commons for which some sort of policy or answer must be improvised. The one thing that is hardly ever discussed is general policy. Nothing, indeed, is more calculated to make a Cabinet Minister unpopular with his colleagues, to cause him to be regarded by them as "Public Enemy No. 1", than a tiresome insistence on discussing general issues of policy, often controversial, when there are so many urgent matters of detail always waiting to be decided. The result is that there is very little Cabinet policy, as such, on any subject. No one has time to think it out, to discuss it, to co-ordinate its various elements, or to see to its prompt and consistent enforcement. There are only departmental policies. The "normal" Cabinet is really little more than a standing conference of departmental chiefs where departmental policies come up, from time to time, to be submitted to a cursory criticism as a

[5] *Thoughts on the Constitution,* by L. S. Amery. London: Oxford University Press, 1947, pp. 86–88.
* *The Forward View,* by L. S. Amery. London: G. Bles, 1935, pp. 443–45.

result of which they may be accepted, blocked, or in some measure adjusted to the competing policies of other departments. But to a very large extent each department goes its own way, following its own bent and its own tradition, fighting the "Whitehall War" to the best of its ability. . . .

'The whole system is one of mutual friction and delay with, at best, some partial measure of mutual adjustment between unrelated policies. It is quite incompatible with any coherent planning of policy as a whole, or with the effective execution of such a policy. It breaks down hopelessly in a serious crisis where clear thinking over difficult and complex situations, definite decisions (not formulae of agreement) and swift and resolute action are required.'

The same conclusion was summed up by the late Professor Ramsay Muir in the following passage of his *How Britain is Governed:*

'The Cabinet has arrogated to itself, half blindly, a series of colossal responsibilities which it cannot meet, which it will not allow Parliament to tackle, and which are not met at all except in so far as they are assumed by the bureaucracy behind the cloak of Cabinet omnipotence.'

Furthermore, Mr. Amery says that with institution of the Cabinet Secretariat with its agenda and its minutes—the flora and fauna of institutionalism—the Prime Minister feels obliged to take up matters of great political importance (specifically, any discussion of the dissolution of Parliament) outside the Cabinet. He also says that no votes are taken and that the Prime Minister states the consensus. He does not, I hasten to add, regret the existence of the Secretariat. He merely indicates that it is not a cure for all evils, although it has done a great work in some fields.

The problem in the United States is not how to provide the Cabinet with a secretariat, but how to improve the ways in which the President brings about teamwork among his departments, and between them and the various parts of his Executive Office.

The creation of the Executive Office of the President in 1939 gave the Presidency a secretariat for the first time in history. The Executive Office, which now includes the White House Office, the Bureau of the Budget, and the Council of Economic Advisers, has greatly increased the range of Presidential direction of departmental policies. The main drive for a "Cabinet secretariat" will always come from persons, including Cabinet members, who have been restive under such Presidential direction, and inclined to seek political support for their independent departmental courses of action.

Nevertheless, on the most important current issues of policy, it is probably true that the President could increase his coordination of departments by establishing a more systematic method for consulting groups of department and agency heads, and for developing a unified Administration-wide approach before the departments begin to compete for their several policies. To do this, the President would need the help of only a small, new-type staff unit within his Executive Office, which he might constitute informally by making use of present members of his Executive Office staff.

A great deal of effort that is now wasted on interdepartmental competition (administrative and political) could be saved if there were a more systematic means of bringing together the department heads concerned with a certain problem and, if possible, getting them to agree. Such a system would present the facts and the departments' views to the President, so that he could either approve (or reverse) their consensus, or consider their disagreement and issue appropriate instructions.

The mechanics and procedures by which this could be done would not be too difficult to work out. More important than any detail of organization and procedure, however, is the general approach. If the President merely permitted groups of his subordinates to establish a system of this nature, it would probably work to his disadvantage. But if the President personally studied the problem and decided to work on some issues through a new type of Presidential policy committees and a slight extension of Presidential staff, he might increase his administrative coordination and the unity of governmental policy.

The President, for example, might have one of his administrative assistants (or other Executive Office staff member) head a small secretariat to serve each of the most important present interdepartmental committees. (For some committees it might seem adequate to have a staff member of the Executive Office serve as an observer on the committee rather than as its secretary.)

The President could then, whenever it seemed desirable, alter the jurisdiction or membership of any committee, and see that its work was properly related to that of other committees. He would probably find it useful to assign most problems not to permanent or continuing committees but to informal *ad hoc* groups. Special care should be taken to see that the President's staff members engaged in work of this type should clear information carefully with other parts of the Executive Office. By this means the President could make sure that the decisions of any continuing or *ad hoc* committee, if he should approve them, would be followed through by all appropriate parts of the Executive Office. By this approach, the President could gradually develop whatever he liked in the way of a system of advisory committees, and he could prevent any encroachment on his position from either the Congress or his own department heads.

Just as the British first saw the need for a more adequate coordination of their policy councils in the fields of defense and foreign affairs, and later transferred to the Cabinet the secretariat first developed in the Committee of Imperial Defence, so the United States Government may well base a more firmly coordinated development of policy on some of the experience of the Executive Committee on Economic Foreign Policy, the

Joint Chiefs of Staff, the State-War-Navy Coordinating Committee, and the Committee of Three (the Secretaries of State, War, and Navy). But if this is to be done without danger to our Constitutional system, it must be done with a full understanding of the differences between Presidential and Cabinet administration. For the President, while he has much less authority than the British Prime Minister, has a much greater burden; he cannot, in the eyes of the people, share his political responsibility for a successful administration with his department heads. Since they do not share his obligations to the people or the party, he cannot share with them control over the procedures by which he obtains their advice.

The Cabinet is not set up so as to be most useful, in an administrative way, to the President. The President might well, with the help of his own staff, advise with and coordinate his department heads in a more systematic yet more flexible manner by providing a Presidential secretariat for the major interdepartmental committees. But any new system must be founded on the same four principles that have always been the basis of the President's Constitutional and administrative relations to his Cabinet: first, he asks to his Cabinet meeting anyone he pleases; second, he has his Cabinet meet whenever he pleases, and discuss any topics he may assign; third, after hearing advice from his Cabinet, the President makes the decision himself on his own personal responsibility; and fourth, the proceedings of the Cabinet are confidential, and may not be called into question in public or before the Congress.

In my excursion into the whole great problem of the President and the Presidency, an excursion which of necessity has explored but an infinitesimal part of the field, I beg the privilege of repeating what I said at the outset: Most of what I have said is based on my own personal observations of the Presidency during the forty-odd years that have elapsed since I first had a conversation in the White House with a President. That particular President, Theodore Roosevelt, was, I think it can be said, the first of the modern Presidents, the first both to induce and to attempt to gratify the great expectations of the people of the United States—expectations that represent their own image of the nation which they compose and which they have created and which they recreate every day. From us, the people, the President needs support as he tries to meet those expectations. He needs sympathy. He needs understanding. He needs patience. But at the same time he needs criticism. He needs to hear our voices. He needs to have us let him know what we think. He needs to have us insist that he tell us what he is thinking, what he is doing, and why. All these things are being better done now and in these later decades than at any previous time.

It were well that they were done even better in the future if we are to accord to the President, as the leader of the nation, the support that he must have from us in his new role as a leader of the world—a role which he cannot avoid unless we, the people, in our turn abdicate the leadership of the United States, the greatest and most powerful of the nations, in the United Nations and in the world.

I would like to say one more thing about the President and the Presidency, and this is addressed in no part to the President but altogether to the people. For 160 years we have made no man President for more than four years at a time. We have freely chosen every four years (and since 1824 we have done it by popular election with an ever-broadening franchise) whomever we pleased to be our President. Now for the first time our freedom of choice is being threatened. An amendment to the Constitution is proposed which for all Presidents except Harry S. Truman would forbid a third term. What this proposal really means, of course, is that after Truman we shall tie our own hands and we will not be free to make our own choice of a man for President. Just as I believe the President should have authority commensurate with his responsibility, so I believe that we, the people, should retain the power and the authority commensurate with our responsibility, to permit the people of the United States of America to choose any person they wish to be their President, and that we do not now forfeit and foreclose the free expression of the will of the people who will be citizens of the United States of America when all of us now living are numbered among the dead.

During the forty-odd years of my looking over the White House fence I have heard every one of its occupants denounced as a despot—even Taft, even Harding, even Coolidge. But, as I have said, in retrospect it is clear that no one of our thirty-two Presidents has even attempted to become a dictator, no one of them has been tainted with Caesarism; all have served in their own way to the best of their hearts and minds the people.

May I read just one more quotation. It is from one of our greatest American novelists, James Fenimore Cooper, but it is not from *The Last of the Mohicans* and not from *The Spy,* not from any one of his fictional works, but from his great political book, *The American Democrat,* published at Cooperstown, New York, in 1838. Wrote James Fenimore Cooper: [6]

As a rule, there is far more danger that the President of the United States will render the office less efficient than was intended, than that he will exercise an authority dangerous to the liberties of the country.

At the root of the distrust of democratic institutions which seems to prevail in many lands and among many peoples today is the fear that popular government cannot hope to be efficient. This fear inclines some countries to accept a system of government that does not rest on the will of the people merely because

[6] *The American Democrat,* by J. Fenimore Cooper. Cooperstown: H. & E. Phinney, 1838. Republished New York: Alfred A. Knopf, Inc., 1931, p. 35.

that system seems to be efficient, seems to be strong. Democracies with their endless debates, their recurring elections, their eternal squabbles, and their floods of talk cannot, so they say, act with either speed or vigor. That these slaves of cynical fears are wrong is the belief of all democrats in all countries and it is the fundamental article of American faith in the American system.

The justification of that faith is instinct in the daily lives of the American people. And that same faith has no greater verification than in the creation, development, and successful operation of that peculiarly American institution—the Presidency.